THE
BRILLIANT
HOME
BUYER

101 INSIDER TIPS
FOR BUYING A HOME
IN THE NEW ECONOMY

KATIE SEVERANCE

ISBN: 978-0-578-75026-2

CONTENTS

PART 2: Finding the Right Home and Making an Offer 57

PART 3: When Your Offer Is Accepted by the Seller — 79

For Jack Severance

Introduction

Long-term homeownership is the most powerful and dependable path to personal wealth for most Americans. Note that the emphasis is on *long-term* — meaning eight to ten years, or more. In fact, this path is so powerful that the sale of a home often funds the retirements of millions of people every year. And of course, homeownership has the added benefit of having provided a roof over their heads and many years of comfort and memories.

By making the choice to buy the right home, in the right location, for the right price, and holding it long-term, you are most definitely putting yourself on the path toward wealth. What else can be bought for only 20% of its value — or less — and then *increase* in value over many years? Cars and boats do not *increase* in value. In fact, they *lose* value the minute you buy them and are almost always sold for a loss. Many stocks and bonds increase in value over the long term, but are most typically bought at 100% of their value.

Because a home is probably the most expensive thing you will ever buy in a lifetime, it can — and should bring you the biggest financial windfall of your life when you sell. To make a brilliant sale in the future, it is critical to make a brilliant buy now. To make a huge profit out of it *tomorrow*, it is crucial that you know what you are doing *today*.

By doing so, you will set yourself up for a day — a day that will definitely come — when having enough money to live on will be the main focus in life. You can bet on that. Some say that a home is not an investment. Technically, that is true. However, if you own a home long term and have made the right choices when buying it, there are very large profits involved when you sell; netting you tens, and in some cases, even hundreds of thousands of dollars.

And yet, in just the past three years, the way we buy homes has completely changed after a century of operating under a slow-paced and predictable business model. The expansion of technology and commerce on the Internet has completely rewritten the rules in real estate. Buyers have more access to information than ever before. Just since 2015, the mortgage industry and lending laws have been re-regulated and re-written. A basic home inspection has become more specialized than ever. The insurance industry continues to adapt to fluctuations in the market and Mother Nature. And we are even at the very beginning stages of using the cryptocurrency Bitcoin to buy and sell real estate.

This book will not just protect you from making costly mistakes before you choose a home and make an offer but also show you how to use smart negotiating strategies. There is no better way to do this than by leveraging the knowledge of a veteran who can share insider knowledge based on two decades of experience and almost $200 million worth of real estate transactions.

In 2010, I co-wrote a book for sellers; *The Complete Idiot's Guide to Selling Your Home*. In the past twenty years, I have also guided buyers in virtually every aspect of the process; over the course of several presidential administrations and in every type of market condition you can imagine — especially the housing crisis of 2008 as well as the Coronavirus pandemic of 2020–21.

There is a lot of information to share, but I wanted to offer it in a very simple and direct manner. So, I have imparted it in tip form. It is designed to be an easy-to-use handbook that you can refer to at any point in the process. This book will be your guide to building long-term wealth through intelligent homeownership.

PART 1

A Broad Real Estate Overview

L et us begin with a brief overview of two of the most important factors to consider for a major purchase like a home — first, how to determine the current state of the real estate market — and second, where mortgage interest rates are hovering.

When to Buy – How's the Market?

The real estate "market" is a fluid thing. It is always moving — at all times. Meaning, the prices (the value) of homes are always changing. The price that a seller can fetch in February could be completely different from the one that he/she could fetch in March. In fact, the price can be different week-to-week and even day-to-day. Think of home values as you would think of a commodity like pork bellies, or cotton and orange juice. The price at which these items trade changes several times in the same day. It's all based on what a buyer is willing to pay at a given moment in time.

Physically, it is the same house in March as it was in February; nothing about the condition has changed except "the market" itself; or what a buyer thinks it's worth.

So, it's very important to know which way the market is moving in your area — is it moving up or down? The answer will not only dictate *when* you should buy, but more importantly, the *speed* at which you should be acting. If the market is going up — meaning sale prices are increasing every month, the longer you wait, the more you will pay. And if it is going down — meaning sale prices are decreasing, then there is less of a sense of urgency.

There are easy-to-understand ways to evaluate the market and they will be covered later in the section called *How to Know the Market*. But also, your real estate agent should be able to illustrate the direction in which the market is heading. This is one of many areas where the use of an agent will be invaluable.

What's Going On With Interest Rates?

The interest rate that you can get on a home loan will have a huge impact on the amount of the monthly mortgage payment. So, it's important to know where rates are currently, and in which direction they are expected to go. If interest rates are expected to rise, that is obviously another reason to act quickly because the longer you wait, the more you will pay. In this area, the advice of your bank or lender will be invaluable.

The interest on a home loan is the amount of money that lenders charges you to borrow. In short, it's the cost of borrowing money. Each month, part of your mortgage payment will be made up of an interest payment. We will cover the details of monthly payments in the mortgage section. But note that, like home prices, interest rates on loans are always moving and changing — everyday and even more than once in a day. They shouldn't fluctuate too wildly day-to-day but they can go up or down significantly over the course of a year.

A clear-eyed way to look at interest rates is that — for every full point that interest rates climb, a buyer will lose about 9% buying power. For the sake of argument, let us round that to 10%. If you have been approved for a mortgage based on a purchase price of $400,000 at the *start* of your search — and have been taking your time finding the right home — and interest rates have *risen* one full point in that time, you will now only be able to buy a home with a purchase price of $360,000. Ten percent of $400,000 is $40,000 worth of lost buying power. On the other hand, if rates *fall* by a full point over the course of your search, you will *increase* your buying power by $40,000. Your lender should be able to give you good advice about where interest rates are headed, and how fast they might change, just as your real estate agent should be able to do the same with the real estate market.

The Pandemic of 2020–21 and Real Estate

The global pandemic of 2020–21 is having a profound effect on the real estate market in many regions of the United States and around the world. The effect has been felt most powerfully in — and just outside of cities. Because of the nature and close proximity of city living, thousands of city dwellers have fled to suburban and rural communities in an effort to feel less exposed to communicable disease and to have more physical space while the work-from-home dynamic is in effect. Many Americans have also sought homes that allow for multi-generational living, to keep the entire family together, safe and not isolated from one another.

For years prior to the pandemic of 2020, housing trends skewed heavily toward urban living, or what's called "vertical" living (think apartments and condos). Americans were moving into cities in droves, looking for simpler living in the form of a shorter commute to work, a smaller space to maintain, lower energy costs, and more of a walkable lifestyle. Many, if not most, housing experts thought this trend would be permanent and even irreversible. The pandemic certainly flipped that notion on its ear. Suddenly, home prices in suburbs outside of cities are skyrocketing, in real time, as of this writing. There is hardly enough supply to meet the demand, and this is causing bidding wars and fast-rising prices. This may change again or even reverse itself.

Some people believe that the real estate market almost always changes suddenly and without warning. And in fact, the pandemic did have a sudden and immediate impact. But, the pandemic aside, many economists and investors don't buy that and claim that there are always tell-tale signs of a changing market. I think there are always signs, too — if you watch the market closely and know what to look for.

The pandemic will end one day and so will its immediate effect on real estate. What lasting impact it will have on real estate remains to be seen and also depends on the "new workplace" and how companies choose to manage employees and the use of office space when all of this is behind us.

What does this mean for you — a potential home buyer? It's a very powerful reminder that it is more important than ever to make a smart buy and avoid overpaying. Of course, it's always important to avoid overpaying but when the market is *up*, it is absolutely critical. It doesn't mean you shouldn't buy. It means you have to be smarter than the rest of the buyer pool. You may decide to rent and wait until a hot real estate market cools down. But note that renting, and not owning, can have an adverse effect on your longterm wealth and finances, as well. Money spent on rent is "after tax" money. You will not be building equity in an asset over time. And *time* is the key ingredient for wealth building. Sure, you won't have to spend money maintaining a home since you don't own it and are not responsible for it. But again, if you make the right buy for the right price, negotiate a good deal for yourself, and hold it longterm, you will make far, far more money in the long run than renting.

The New "Know Before You Owe" Laws

Before 2015, if you were shopping for a home loan and you spoke to a lender, they would give you an estimate of the fees you could expect to pay. It was called a *Good Faith Estimate* of costs. But it was a very confusing document and worse, the form varied wildly from one lender to another. This made it nearly impossible to comparison shop and understand the figures given to you.

The good news is that, in 2015, new laws came into effect to protect buyers. They are commonly known as the "Know Before You Owe" laws. As part of the Consumer Financial Protection Bureau (CFPB) oversight, they made the documents more uniform, transparent, and easier to understand. The new document is called a *Loan Estimate* and lenders must give it you, by law, within three days of applying for a loan.

You can take the loan estimate given to you by a bank (or mortgage broker) and compare it side by side with one from another bank in order to see who is giving you the best deal.

Bitcoin and Real Estate

Bitcoin is the most widely used form of cryptocurrency. In recent years, but especially in 2020, it has gained widespread acceptance among many major banks and financial institutions. We are also learning, from recent statistics shared by Schwab, that Millennials are embracing Bitcoin as one of the top five holdings in their retirement accounts.

Known as "the internet's money," Bitcoin is following the typical path of monetary adoption. First as a collectible; then as a store of value. The adoption of Bitcoin will occur gradually — and then appear to be sudden as consumers become more accustomed to using digital currency for their day-to-day purchases.

At some point, as the price of Bitcoin continues to go up, adoption will pick up and will create more of a need for it as a medium of exchange. In real estate, this will likely happen first at the ultra-high-end of the market and in global cities where interested parties are highly sophisticated.

However, one day — in my opinion, there will be many sellers who will price their homes in Bitcoin as a way to gain exposure to the cryptocurrency, and/or to attract a wealthy Bitcoin buyer. Despite the fact that some transactions have already happened with Bitcoin, it will be some time before its use in real estate becomes commonplace. Some title companies — and other real estate related companies, are already looking for ways to use "blockchain technology" to make the process of buying and selling real estate more stream-lined. But for now, people who own Bitcoin are a unique market unto themselves and it is still hard for most buyers and sellers to wrap their minds around using digital money for the purchase or sale of something as large as a home.

Climate Change and Real Estate

Many buyers may think that climate change is seen mainly in higher tides and floods in coastal areas. But the banks and insurance companies see climate change affecting homes in many different ways; not just on the coasts, and not just from water. There is basic inland flooding, river flood plains, flammable canyons, mountainsides susceptible to brush fire, earthquake zones, tornado alleys, hurricane zones, and even tsunami washout zones.

If you buy a home in a beautiful but high-risk area, there are many types of weather-resistant technologies that can be employed, and they do not have to be too expensive. Ask questions about what risks are common to your area and what modifications can make a home more resistant to the effects of climate change in the region. There are special insurance policies available, as well. These steps don't eliminate the risk but they can make it manageable.

There are areas where rising sea levels, hurricanes, brush fires, earthquakes, and tornadoes pose a risk that can be anticipated — to some degree. It is important to educate yourself about them and how they impact local housing. Do as much research as you can, and have conversations with the professionals you are working with — your real estate agent, insurance carrier, title company, and home inspector. Actually, insurance professionals are a great source because these companies evaluate risk for a living.

How to Begin the Process of Buying a Home

The process of buying a home can be intimidating and feel complicated, especially to a first time buyer. The good news is that the steps in the process do not happen all at once. They are sequential and predictable. If you approach them one at a time, thoughtfully, you will feel less stress, avoid costly mistakes, and will make an absolutely brilliant buy — and therefore a brilliant sale, one day.

Information-Gathering Mode and the Biggest Change in the World of Real Estate

The number one change in real estate is the speed and availability of information on the Internet. As a result, you no longer need the assistance of a professional to *begin* a search. You do not need to make a single phone call or take one meeting to begin looking for a home. Eventually, you will. Soon enough, you will need to rely on the help of several different types of professionals. Some services will be for free; others will cost money. But for now, *you* are your own team because you begin the whole process in "information-gathering" mode. And thanks to the Internet, much of the information you need to "gather" is right at your fingertips. You can begin online, and proceed at your own pace, until you are ready to get really serious.

This information-gathering period could last weeks or months, depending on your motivation. It would not be wrong to speak with lenders, lawyers, and real estate agents at the outset but it is just not necessary until you have done some thinking about *where* you want to live and if you are really ready to become a homeowner. The answers to these two major questions are usually found by talking it over with family, a spouse or partner, or close friends, and through some good old fashioned self-reflection about where you are in your life, where you want to go, and how fast you'd like to get there. Later, when you are serious about buying, the pace will automatically pick up and the professionals will become involved.

How to Choose the Right Community: The Most Important Mistake to Avoid

One of the biggest mistakes to avoid is picking the wrong community. And it happens more often than you would think. A city, town, or community has many layers to it. It is important to peel back the layers and spend time investigating it beyond just driving through and looking at properties.

Take your time in this stage and do your research. Do not choose a town just because it is pretty, or warm and sunny. Or because someone you know lives there and says it is a great place to live. Or because you saw a great property online and drifted into some random public open house and fell in love with the kitchen.

You can always renovate a home, or move from one street to another *within* the community. But, if you pick the wrong town, you put yourself and your family in a very tough spot.

You will have to pull children out of school and start all over in an entirely new area which is a difficult and expensive thing to do — financially and emotionally. Or worse, your circumstances may prevent you from relocating. You will have to stay in a community that you may grow to dislike more and more. Consider the choice of a community to be the most important of any real estate decision you will make.

Tip #01   Access: What the Region Should Offer

A major change in real estate is that people are measuring the quality of life by looking at the living *experience*. More than ever, homes are most valuable in towns that connect people to jobs, transportation, health care, and recreation.

For example, many home buyers are no longer willing to spend more than forty-five to fifty minutes commuting to work each way; and they want access to weekend recreation that does not require too much travel.

So, what can you get to if you drove fifteen to sixty minutes in any direction from the town you are considering? Strongly consider communities with direct access to some type of a metropolitan area and/or corporate hub, at least one major highway or commuter train line, and a good hospital. Even better — if you can get to a recreation area in under an hour, you have done really well. It could be a beach, national park, ski resort, fishing and boating, theme park or a major zoo.

Rural or Country Living

All this talk of "access" is not to say that one should not buy a house in an extreme rural area — especially when these areas offer some of the most beautiful land in the nation. Rural life can be hugely rewarding for people who dislike crowds and cities. The affordability, space, and natural beauty are perks. But, do keep in mind that you would still need reasonable access to health care, at the least. It is important to check out the availability of both routine and emergency medical care, as well as trauma care options.

Economic Stability

If a community (or region) is economically unstable, and could possibly get worse, you could lose much of the value of any home you buy, no matter how much you improve it or beautify it. It's important to understand the state of the local economy; if it is stable; if the people who live there are able to work, to hang onto their jobs, and if businesses are surviving. On the other hand, later on we will discuss how to spot a town or neighborhood that is *increasing* in value. If the area around your home is becoming more valuable overall (for a variety of reasons), this will typically have a far greater impact on the value of your home than if you gut-renovated the entire kitchen — and it won't cost you a dime. Simply by being smarter and choosing wisely — by buying in the right place and at the right time, you could gain tens of thousands of dollars in extra equity in your home. And in some parts of the country where great change is happening, it could even be hundreds of thousands of dollars.

So, look into the economic stability of the region by asking a few questions. If the area happens to be remote or isolated, is the population stable? Is it growing or shrinking? Are more people moving in or moving out? Is the entire region supported by one big corporation that employs a majority of the residents? What would happen to the community if that corporation closed its doors?

Asking around — and a little research, goes a long way.

Crime and Infamy
How to Do a Deep Dive into a Town's History

Real estate agents are not allowed to discuss crime statistics with you. You will need to do your own research and due diligence on this subject. You can visit or call the local police station. And sometimes crime statistics can be found online.

When you search the name of the community online, often all that comes up is the town website or the school board site. You need to dive deeper.

Sometimes a community is "infamous" for something bad that happened there – something that a real estate agent is not required, or even allowed, to discuss. The best source for information like this is probably the website of the newspaper in the nearest major city – not the local paper. And there may not even be a local paper. Even if there is one, it may underplay a tragedy, a major crime, or an environmental problem. A big paper in a big nearby city will almost always cover a major incident or condition in a nearby town or suburb.

You can also drop in on podcasts and live town council meetings to see what is going on locally.

Tip #02   The Culture: Find Your People

The culture is a combination of the vibe and the values of a community. What are the people like? Read the local paper online. See if there is a local social network — that is an excellent place to read comments and see what the residents say about and to one another. Are there places for arts and entertainment? Are the people there civic minded and involved? Is the local government running well? Is the town council effective and not dysfunctional? Stop by the town hall and ask a question or two and see how they treat you.

Some towns have a strong political leaning in one way or another. Find out if it is liberal or conservative. Politics have creeped into our everyday lives in a way that did not exist a decade ago. And this can affect your day-to-day life. If you are a conservative in a very liberal town, or vice versa, you might want to learn this before you have bought a home there.

Tip #03 — Property Taxes: High or Low? Either Way, They Can Tell You an Awful Lot

If the taxes are high, it could reflect amazing services. But it can also reflect a poorly run government, a budget that is not balanced, or municipal debt — or all three. Some towns get into financial trouble (debt) because they float bonds — a kind of borrowing — to make infrastructure repairs and improvements. Sometimes, the taxes are just higher because the township provides more (and better) services than others. As the saying goes, you get what you pay for.

On the other hand, if the taxes are very low, find out why that is. Some communities do not have a public sewer system. Instead, each home has its own septic system that is operated at the sole cost of the homeowner. Some towns do not have garbage pickup, expecting homeowners to deliver their garbage or recyclables to the local dump. How big is the police force? Is there a viable fire department or does the town share one with a neighboring community? Is there an ambulance service? Is the school system well-funded? There is often a direct connection between low taxes and fewer municipal services.

Tip #04 — School District: It Is Not Just about Test Scores Anymore

Many websites (and there are plenty of them) rank school districts based solely on test scores. But, test scores no longer tell the whole story of a district and this is another big change in recent years. A sample Google search will bring up several sites. Make sure you look at how each website *actually* ranks.

Some districts have lower average test scores because the community is economically and culturally diversified. This may be a sign of a strong, inclusive school system. Remember, it is just an *average*. It does not mean that the school district is not producing Ivy League-caliber graduates. Many towns publish a list each year, of colleges and universities that their graduates have been accepted to. That list a great gauge of the caliber of the local school system.

Another sign of a strong district is whether or not it provides services for students with ADHD (Attention Deficit Hyperactive Disorder) and other learning disabilities, as well as a healthy selection of AP (advanced placement) classes for advanced students. These types of services require great teachers. And great teachers and services cost money. If they are provided, it is sign of a strong district and you should consider this when looking at the rankings.

Tip #05 Parks and Recreation: Huge Impact on Value

This is obviously a very important quality-of-life issue, but good parks and recreation programs will dramatically improve the value of your home over time. Even if you do not plan to use them, these amenities will matter a great deal when you sell the property. Beautiful parks and recreation are an important lifestyle feature and appeal to everyone.

Observe how well the parks are maintained. Do they have good, clean playgrounds for the little ones? Dog parks? Bike paths? Do the streets have bike lanes? Is there a public swimming pool? Tennis courts? Skating rink? Access to hiking and kayaking? Town fireworks on the Fourth of July? Sports leagues? A YMCA? The more amenities there are, the more value is added to every home in the community.

ONLINE SHOPPING AND PUBLIC OPEN HOUSES

Tip #06   Everything Begins Online: What Is Your Taste?

This is one of the biggest changes of all in real estate. As you are well aware, you can "virtually" walk through a hundred homes on the Internet. This is how most buyers begin a search and how they decide what they like — and what it will cost them. Statistically, home buyers spend weeks or months shopping for properties online before they hire an agent or choose a lender to get pre-approved for a loan.

If you are married or have a partner, this is the best and the fastest way to find out if you share the same vision about style, architecture, and location. This is no small thing. I have worked with hundreds of couples who have had to work through a difference of opinion about these things. It always gets worked out in the end and they come to an agreement. But it is important to investigate, and the easiest way to do that is by browsing together first, from the comfort of your home.

Tip #07   Pick the *Right* Multiple Listing Service: They Are Not All Created Equal

Have you ever called a real estate agent about a house, only to learn that it is already under contract? It happens all the time. You might be surprised to learn that some of the most well-known real estate sites are often inaccurate, featuring out-of-date, and in some cases, bogus listings.

Here is a trick: there are *private* regional MLSs, used *only* by agents. They are the most accurate and reliable. And many of them have a *public* site that is connected, in real time, to the private site. Ask an agent which ones they use, and let them direct you to the best site.

When all else fails, in my opinion, the most accurate national public site is realtor.com. It is owned by Realtors and is connected to professional MLSs.

Once you choose an agent to work with, getting accurate up-to-the-minute information will no longer be a challenge because you will receive listings directly from the agent and the information will be 100% reliable.

Tip #08   Public Open Houses: Use the Host Agent to Get Info You Cannot Get Online

Many buyers walk through the open house and want nothing to do with the host agent. They do not even want to make eye contact unless they have to. I understand this because buyers know that the agent is trying to either sell you the house or get you as a client and sell you a home in the future.

But lean into it! You do not have to agree to work with that agent in order to simply chat. Use the agent to your advantage. Educate yourself about renovations, taxes and land use, amenities, public and private schools nearby, etc. Ask the agent's opinion about which way the market might be headed, how much it costs to make certain improvements, which schools his/her kids go to and why, if there are any pending municipal assessments, any imminent new construction, or the best commuting routes.

These pieces of information and opinions will differ from agent to agent, so, ask questions in every open house. Compare the responses to get the real story.

LOCK 'N' LEAVE LIFESTYLE: BUYING A CONDOMINIUM OR COOPERATIVE (CO-OP) INSTEAD OF A HOUSE

Buying a condominium or a co-op is appealing to some buyers because they are usually much less expensive than a house. There is less physical upkeep to think about. This kind of ownership is sometimes referred to as "Lock 'n' Leave" because it allows you to come and go without worrying about maintenance, except for a few appliances inside the unit. On the other hand, there are also quite a few unique considerations (and extra fees) that would not otherwise apply if you were buying a regular house. When you apply for a loan to buy a condo or a co-op, a lender will take the added expenses into consideration.

Maintenance Fees or HOA Fees

When you own a house, you will make monthly payments to cover:

- property taxes

- homeowner's insurance

- mortgage payment

But when you own a condo or co-op, you will have all these expenses, plus a monthly fee collected by the building's Condominium Association, Co-op Board, or Homeowner's Association (HOA), which hires, oversees, and pays contractors to maintain the common areas. It is called a maintenance fee but is also referred to as an HOA fee. While most of this fee goes toward upkeep of the property, it can also be used to pay for utilities, limited insurance, and property improvements, and to make contributions to the building's capital reserves.

Tip #09 Look at Capital Reserves and the Balance Sheet

Basically, you need to know if the building has a healthy capital reserve. In other words, are they putting enough money in the bank for emergency repairs and upgrades? The more money they have saved up in capital reserves, the steadier the value of the building will be and the more protected you will be — as an owner, from the building getting into financial trouble or debt. A good target for condo associations is to be able to direct at least 25% of all maintenance fees to the reserve fund.

Things can go wrong in a building. It might need a new roof, or a central air-conditioning system, or maybe the parking lot needs to be repaved. If there is not enough money in the reserves, then the condo or co-op board will vote to impose an *assessment* on all unit owners. This is a fixed amount charged to you each month until the repair or improvement is paid for.

You have the right to ask for the building's balance sheet and financials before you commit to buying a unit. But unless you know how to read financial disclosures, buying a condo or co-op is the type of purchase that definitely calls for the advice of a full-time real estate attorney, in my opinion.

Existing, Imminent, or Possible Assessments

It is important to know if there are any assessments in place for repairs or improvements in the building or on the property. *Existing assessments* are well documented, so it is not hard to find out about them. *Imminent assessments* have not taken effect yet but they are at least known and will take effect at some point in the near future. These are sometimes documented before you buy, but not always. *Possible assessments* are the hardest to research because they may only be in the discussion stage and may not ever happen. But you should still know about them before you buy. One way to find out if there is a possible assessment looming on the horizon, is to ask for copies of the minutes from past board meetings.

Tip #10 Ask for Copies of Past Board Meeting Minutes

Many unit owners do not bother to attend the building's board meetings that are open to all. So, the seller may not be up-to-date and informed about what is really going on with future plans for the building. And if your seller does not know that a major upgrade or repair is in the discussion stage, then he/she cannot disclose it to you. That is how possible future assessments slip through the cracks and take you by surprise *after* you have bought a unit.

Always ask for copies of the minutes from past condo or co-op board meetings. Go back at least six months, assuming the board meets monthly. If the board only meets quarterly, then ask for at least a year's worth. The minutes are pretty easy to read and understand. Reading the minutes is not just about upcoming projects and possible assessments — you also want know if the board is effective and efficient and not dysfunctional.

What Type of Ownership Are You Buying Into?

When you buy a house, the legal type of ownership is called *fee simple*. This means you are the sole owner of both the land and the building. You can do whatever you want to it, provided your choices comply with local ordinances.

Condos

Buying a condominium offers a different kind of ownership. You will own your unit entirely, but *only* from the walls inward. But you will also *share* ownership in everything from the walls outward: the land on which the building sits and common areas (aka common elements) such as hallways, lobby, basement, laundry room, communal garage or parking lot, swimming pool, tennis courts, walkways, paths, and lawn.

Your "shared ownership" in these areas is referred to as having an undivided interest in the common elements. So, in addition to owning your unit, you have a shared responsibility and stake in maintaining the rest of the property. You are required to help pay for this through the monthly maintenance fee or HOA fee. Keeping the common areas in good condition will only help preserve the value of both the building and your unit. At the time of your purchase, you want to be assured that the common areas have been well-cared for in the past and that they will continue to be in the future.

Deed and Property Taxes: With a condo, you will be given your own individual deed and your own individual property tax bill.

Co-Op's Stock Certificate in Lieu of Deed: When you buy a cooperative (co-op) it is slightly more complicated. You do not receive a deed but rather a stock certificate that shows that you own a number of shares, or an interest, in the co-op building (or complex). You will also receive what is called a proprietary lease from the co-op association, as well as a bill of sale for your unit.

Property Taxes: With a co-op, you do not receive a tax bill; nor do you pay your own property taxes directly to the municipality. Your portion of property taxes are included in the maintenance fee. For this reason, co-op maintenance fees often appear to be much higher than condo maintenance fees.

The reason the taxes are paid as part of the maintenance fees is because there is only one tax bill for the entire co-op building. The portion of taxes that you owe depends on the number of shares you own. And the number of shares you own depends mostly on the size (square footage) of the unit you are buying.

Co-op Boards Can Reject You

Another issue to consider when buying a co-op is that you will probably need to fill out a pretty lengthy application package which is then submitted to the co-op board for approval. As a result, they can reject you without giving a reason.

They will ask for all kinds of information about your background, job, and personal finances. The Board members will review your application and approve or reject you, based on the application package. The board may also require that you appear before them for an in-person interview. This process can take longer than other kinds of real estate purchases because board members usually do not meet more than once a month, at most. You can sometimes wait two or three months for the board to issue its final verdict on you, and this can delay the closing.

If You Feel You Have Been a Victim of Discrimination

- Both the federal government and state governments regulate housing discrimination. The federal laws are part of the Fair Housing Act, which forbids discrimination against buyers and tenants on the basis of race, religion, national origin, sex, family status, or disability.
- Individual state laws can be much more stringent than the federal laws, covering additional types of discrimination, including the ones on the basis of age, marital status, and sexual orientation.
- If you feel that your rights have been violated, you are encouraged to file a complaint with both the appropriate agency within your state and the federal agency, i.e., the Fair Housing and Urban Development Agency, better known as HUD.

Buying a Multi-Family Home Instead of a Single Family

Tip #11

The Most Powerful Wealth Strategy: To Owner-Occupy (live in) Your Multi-Family — At Least at First!

Of all the paths to wealth, owning an income-producing property, and living in it, is the most powerful by far. I am talking about a multi-family house or a small building with two to four apartments under the same roof.

Investment properties used to be bought mostly by professional investors or very savvy people who were bullish on real estate. All that has changed now. The secret is out on the power of passive income. Millions of people are snatching up investment properties all over the world.

But many investors may not want, or be able, to live in them. They buy them as an asset only for the investment income. However, if you are able to live in the home, the loan will be easier to get and you will save money both today and for as long as you own it. The reason is that lenders require a larger down payment for investment properties when the buyer/investor does not live in it. If you choose to live in it, as your primary residence, you can put less money down now (preserving your cash), get a lower interest rate — and therefore pay far less in total interest over the course of the loan.

Even if you can live there for only the first year or two, not only will you have provided a roof over your head but you will also have collected passive income from the tenant(s) This will dramatically reduce your own monthly living expenses — maybe even by half! And by living on the premises, you can do maintenance and small improvements much more easily.

You can always move out at some later date and replace yourself with another renter and use that added income to pay for the total carrying costs. Then hold the property for years, collecting passive income — until the day you are ready to sell. It is important to notify your lender and insurance carrier if and when you move out.

Can You Afford a Multi-Family Property?

If you are concerned that a two or three-family home is too expensive and that you will not qualify for a bigger loan, think again. If you make the right buy, the rental income will cover all of the monthly carrying costs. To put it another way, you should not be buying any investment property that does not completely pay for itself each and every month. That is the whole point — to buy something that not only pays for itself but also provides you with extra income after you have covered the monthly and annual expenses.

Furthermore, the bank is more likely to approve you for the bigger loan because you are seen as having two streams of income: one from your day job and the other from your tenant(s).

For example, let us say you buy a two-family home and the total expenses are $2,000 per month. If you live in one unit and your tenant is living in the other unit and paying you $1,200 per month in rent, you are only responsible for coming up with another $800 per month to cover your monthly carrying costs. And all the while, you will own an asset that will appreciate over the long term. If you had bought a single-family home, your monthly payments could be twice that and there is no tenant to offset or help you make mortgage, insurance, and property tax payments.

Should You Buy a Multi-Family Property?

Owning a multi-family is not very different from owning a home in terms of maintaining it and paying property taxes and the monthly mortgage. You will have the same responsibilities — whether you buy a single-family home or a multi-family home. But there are two major differences.

The first big difference is that a considerable portion of the mortgage, taxes, and maintenance expenses will be paid by your tenant(s). That's good!

The second big difference is that you will become a landlord. This may not be so good, depending on your perspective. It is not hard to learn how to become a landlord, but it does require constant time and attention. Some months will be very easy and you will not have to lift a finger; the checks will come pouring in. But in other months, it may feel like a part-time job, taking a few hours of your time to deal with tasks and troubleshoot problems. If you can handle that, owning a multi-family is well worth it.

Finding and Keeping Tenants

It is obviously important to keep the other unit (or units) rented, so that your cash flow is steady. You will need to find good, responsible tenants. This can be a yearly chore if you do not luck out with great long-term tenants who will stay for a few years. However, a real estate agency can advertise your rental, find and vet good candidates for you, draw up the leases, and get background checks performed. In many areas, the tenant pays the commission for rentals so you may be able to get these real estate services for free. If this is the case, then it is truly a great thing because a professional will take this task entirely off your plate — at no expense to you.

If you want to find tenants on your own, it is going to be slightly harder. You will need to list the rental on the MLSs, respond to inquiries, show the unit, and vet tenants yourself — which will take time out of your day. You can ask for a reference letter from a past landlord, proof of employment, and/or income in the form a recent pay stub, or a letter from the company that the tenant works for. Many landlords require credit checks to be done while others require full-blown background checks. But again, if a real estate agency is involved, this can all be done for you.

As the landlord, you will still need to collect rent each month and be responsive to the tenants' needs in terms of repairs or problems. Tenants can sometimes be troublesome if they are noisy, do not follow rules or fail to pay their rent on time. So, there are some stressors, indeed when managing tenants. A good, neat, clean, quiet, long-term, reliable tenant is worth his/her weight in gold.

Investor-Owned vs. Owner-Occupied Multi-unit Buildings

Your lender will want to know what percentage of the building's units are owner-occupied. A building that houses a lot of renters is not as attractive nor as valuable as a building with mostly owner-occupied units. You may have guessed that this is because owner-occupied units will be better maintained and cared for than units occupied by renters. This makes the investment safer for the lender. When a unit is occupied by a renter, it is considered to be investor-owned. If more than 50% of the units are investor-owned, this can have a negative impact on the valuation of the building and therefore on your ability to get a loan, and even on your ability to refinance it after you own.

DEFINITION: *Passive Income*
Passive income is money that comes to you from an investment, in either a rental property or a business in which you do not "materially partici-pate." In other words, you do not have to do much to collect the income.

Tip #12	How to Make a Brilliant Multi-Family Purchase

The key to making a killing with an income-producing property is to make the right purchase from the outset. To do that, the you must keep a keen eye on the basic math and also consider the qualities and amenities of a potentially profitable multi-family. How much profit will hinge on being able to get the highest rent possible from tenants. So, you need to know the math associated with the purchase of the building, but also understand what tenants are looking for in a rental.

The math basically comes down to three numbers:

- GOI: Gross Operating Income

- TOE: Total Operating Expenses

- NOI: Net Operating Income

Gross Operating Income is the total potential rental income on the property. How much rent can you expect to get? This should be provided to you by the seller, the listing agency, or the fact that at least one of the units is already rented, so you will know for sure what you can get. If there are two units in the building (a two-family) renting for $1,300 each, then the total monthly rent is $2,600.

To get the GOI, you calculate $2,600 × 12 months = $31,200.

Total Operating Expenses are the annual costs to cover maintenance (repairs, lawn care, snow removal), utilities, insurance, property taxes, etc., but not the mortgage payment. Let us say, these expenses total to about $12,000 a year.

Net Operating Income is what you get when you subtract the TOE from the GOI.

GOI ($31,200) − TOE ($12,000) = NOI ($19,200)

This means that you have $19,200 each year to apply to the mortgage payments. If your annual mortgage payments total $15,000 for the year, then you have a positive cash flow (net profit) of $4,200 — annually. The two family asset is not only completing paying for itself every year, but it is "throwing off" or earning you an extra $4,200 a year as profit in the form of passive income. This profit is taxable but there are ways to reduce that amount in the eyes of the IRS and this passive income is taxed differently than active income from your regular job.

Depreciation

Note that when you file your taxes, you will be able to write off some of the annual profit using a legally allowable expense called *depreciation*. This is a tax law that allows you to offset income from an investment property — each and every year that you own it, by claiming "wear and tear" and physical deterioration of the property. Consult your tax accountant for specifics, but this is a commonly used tax loophole.

Important Amenities and Traits to Consider When Buying a Multi-Family Property

There is more to think about than just the numbers when buying a multi-family or other income-producing property. Every question is driven by the main goal, which is to maximize the rent you can get from tenants. Ask yourself what amenities you would pay a little extra for if you were a tenant.

- **Is there a laundry room on premise or would the tenants have to go to a laundromat?** It is not that expensive to install a washer/dryer in the basement, (or in each unit if there is room). And not having to take their laundry off-site is a big time-saver and makes an enormous difference to tenants.
- **Are shops and public transportation nearby?** The ability to walk to shops and a commuter bus or train is a huge draw for tenants and they will almost always pay a premium for it — especially if they do not have a car.
- **Is there parking on the property?** For tenants who own a car, this is a highly desirable amenity, especially in cities where parking is almost always limited and finding convenient and affordable off-site parking is a major hassle.
- **Are there separate entrances for each unit?** This is a big added value as well for the tenant but also for you, if you live on premises. Having your own entrance is a luxury and offers privacy which isn't always available in a communal living situation.

Historic Homes

Buying a home that is designated as historic — or even buying one that is just located within a historic district can seem charming. But there may be restrictions on what changes you can make to the exterior. Many towns have historic preservation organizations that hold the power to control renovations and/or changes to these types of homes. Make sure you investigate what you can and cannot do, if you decide to buy one.

GETTING A MORTGAGE IN THE NEW ECONOMY

When you make an offer on a home, you will need to prove to the seller that you have qualified for a home loan (mortgage) — unless, of course you are paying with all cash, which is rare. You prove this by applying to a bank or a lender for a *mortgage pre-approval*. When the lender pre-approves you, they will issue you a *pre-approval letter* to attach to any offer you make. Without one, most sellers, and their real estate agent or attorney, are not likely to take your offer seriously.

The process of getting a mortgage has greatly changed since the housing crisis of 2008, when nearly anyone, even those buyers with poor credit, could get approved for a loan. Today, it is still possible to get a loan if your credit is not that good, or if you do not have a lot of money saved for the down payment. But the guidelines have become stricter.

The New Lending Laws

The good news is that, thanks to the new "Know Before You Owe" laws, the process of shopping for a loan has now become more transparent and easier for buyers to navigate and understand.

As discussed in the overview of this book, these new laws came into effect in 2015 to protect buyers. They are part of the Consumer Financial Protection Bureau (CFPB) oversight, and they made lending documents more uniform, transparent, and simple to understand. Before 2015, when you were shopping for a loan among different lenders, each one gave you their own form — called a *"Good Faith Estimate"* which outlined their terms and the cost of borrowing. The problem was that these forms were extremely confusing and each bank used a different format. It was impossible to effectively comparison shop. So a new one was created — called a *Loan Estimate*. It is a uniform document now used by all lenders — and, the lenders must give it you, by law, within three days after applying for a loan.

Now, you can take the Loan Estimate given to you by one bank (or mortgage broker) and compare it side by side with one from another bank, in order to see who is giving you the best deal.

Once you choose a lender, <u>keep the Loan Estimate handy until you are about to close on the property</u> and compare it to the Closing Disclosure Form that you will be given just before closing, to be sure that the final figures closely match the ones they gave you at the outset. If they do not match, the lender needs to explain why. (More on this in the closing section)

PITI: The Four Parts of a Mortgage Payment

Most buyers start the borrowing process by first deciding how much money they can afford to spend *per month*, in the form of a mortgage payment. A monthly mortgage payment is made up of four parts. The acronyms to help you remember it is "PITI".

PITI stands for:

- *Principal (the amount borrowed)*

- *Interest (the fee charged each month by the lender; the cost of borrowing)*

- *Taxes (property taxes)*

- *Insurance (homeowner's insurance; can also include PMI — private mortgage insurance)*

Private Mortgage Insurance (PMI)

If you have not saved quite enough money for a 20% downpayment (the gold standard for banks and lenders) you can still buy a home but you may have to pay PMI, or *Private Mortgage Insurance* (unless you qualify for a certain kind of loan like FHA or VA – see loan types). This is an extra fee – added to the monthly payment that provides a kind of insurance for the lender if you cannot pay the loan back. They charge this because, with a lower downpayment, you have less equity (level of ownership) in the home than the bank would like. The bank finances 80% and wants you to have at least 20% ownership or equity in the property. When you put down less, this makes you more of a risk. (See *Loan-to-Value Ratio* in this section) PMI payments can go away over time as your home improves in value (and your own equity in the home increases relative to the bank's equity) or, you choose to make some extra payments along the way until PMI can be removed.

FICO Scores: How to Check Your Credit Status

Your credit score greatly affects your ability to get a loan. The higher the score, the better off you will be. Almost everyone has a late payment or two in their credit history, and that alone can lower your score. Do not worry. Unless you have very serious credit problems (for any number of reasons), you can usually improve your FICO score in a few months. Do it now. Do not wait until you are shopping for a house. While credit problems can be cleared up relatively quickly it does take some time.

You can go to a lender to find out your credit score. If it is too low, they will explain how to clean it up and raise it. They will do this for free because they want your future business.

You can also get your FICO score online through a number of websites that offer free credit reports and scores. But you might not get the same in-depth, personal, one-on-one advice that you would get from an in-person representative.

FICO *(Fair Isaac Corporation)*

The Fair Isaac Corporation is a data analytics company that provides credit score services for just about everyone. It is called a FICO Score, for short, and it has become a fixture in the US consumer lending industry, used by lenders to determine the risk of lending money to an individual.

Tip #13 — How to Interpret Your Credit Score: Poor to Excellent

While there are different companies that issue scores, the FICO score is, by far, the most commonly used by lenders. The score tells lenders how likely you are to pay your bills, and on time. In other words, how good you are at repaying debt. The better your credit score, the better the mortgage products (and interest rates) will be at your disposal.

Credit scores range from 300 to 850 and fall into categories such as poor, good, very good, and exceptional. To make things simple, know that a "good" score falls in 600 and up, and a "very good" or "excellent" score will be well up into the 700s. A score over 800 is considered "exceptional."

Credit scores come from three credit bureaus: Equifax, Experian, and TransUnion. The reports from these bureaus show exactly when and where you have missed or made late payments. The good news is that they are *each* required to make a free report available to you, annually — if you request it.

Tip #14 — The Down Payment: How Much Cash You Will Need (Loan to Value)

Again, the gold standard is to put down at least 20% of the sale price, but it is not always required in order to get a mortgage. Banks call this an 80/20 Loan-to-Value Ratio, or LTV. An 80/20 LTV is the bank's *preference* — to loan you up to 80% of the purchase price.

On a $400,000 home, that is an $80,000 deposit. Do not panic! Not everyone can afford to put that much money down. And that is okay. There are many ways around this and many different types of mortgage products described in the following pages, some requiring as little as 3% down. If you are a military veteran, you can put zero money down — if you meet certain prerequisites.

Tip #15 — Debt-to-Income Ratio: An Important Number to Keep as Low as Possible!

Your debt-to-income ratio (commonly referred to as DTI), is easy to calculate and is an extremely important number to banks because it reflects how much of a risk you are as a borrower and helps to determine how much money they will lend you. But your DTI should also be very important to *you* because buyers are quite often approved to borrow more money than they really should. This is no joke. Banks approving buyers for a loan with a high DTI was one of the causes of the housing crisis of 2008. The whole point of this book is that — for you to make a lot of money selling this home one day in the future, you need to be able to carry it comfortably, without getting into financial trouble along the way.

The DTI is always expressed as a percentage. The lower it is, the more attractive you are to the lender; and the more financially sound you will be in life. Calculating your DTI is a really powerful (and quick) exercise for anyone who is looking at their budget and evaluating their financial security as it relates to owning real estate.

Calculating DTI

DTI is calculated by taking your total monthly debt and dividing it by your gross monthly income — that is, your income *before* taxes and other regular paycheck deductions.

Let us say that your gross monthly income is $5,000 (again, before taxes). Your current rent is $1,100 per month. Your car payment is $300 per month and your student loan is $100 per month. So, your total monthly debt is $1,500 per month. If you divide $1,500 by $5,000, your DTI is 30%, which is good.

Most lenders like to see a DTI between 28 and 33% going just for monthly housing costs. This means that you are spending 28–33% of your pre-tax income *just* on a mortgage payment or rent. Lenders will approve some buyers with a DTI as high as 43%, when they include all monthly debt like car and student loans. So, you can see why a DTI of 30% would look very good to a bank.

That said, just because you can still get approved with a DTI as high as 43% does not mean that you should. Imagine that almost half of your monthly income is going toward paying a mortgage, student loan, car loan, healthcare, etc. — all before paying income taxes, buying food, and other living expenses. To be safe and smart, it's very important that your mortgage payment is low enough so that you can afford to pay it for at least six months if you should lose your job. Even if you don't ever lose your job, having enough money left over each month to be able to save is a key to building wealth — not to mention the reduction in stress which can actually extend your life.

Tip #16   Getting Pre-qualified vs. Pre-approved; The Paperwork You Will Need

You can get pre-qualified for a loan very quickly — sometimes in as little as an hour. But to be fully pre-approved for a loan, you will need to gather more in-depth paperwork, and it takes just a little more time. A pre-qualification allows you to quickly get an idea of what you can afford. But it is not enough proof of your ability to buy a home. A genuine pre-approval means that the bank has fully vetted and evaluated your finances in great detail.

You can usually get *pre-qualified* for a loan by simply providing the lender with:

- Your social security number

- Permission for the lender to run a credit check

- A verbal disclosure of your total debt and total assets

You can get *pre-approved* for a loan by providing more detailed documentation, which includes at least the following:

- A copy of one to two years' worth of tax returns

- A copy of your most recent W-2, or 1099 form

- Recent bank statements

- Recent pay stubs

- A copy of your driver's license and other documents like proof of employment letters, etc.

Do not wait long to begin the pre-approval process. When you wait, you could be looking at homes you cannot really afford. It takes time to pull all the paperwork together. When you find a great home that you are excited to buy, your time and thoughts are consumed by the property itself, and writing up, and submitting the offer. That is not the time to be rushing around trying to organize financial documents, especially if there is another buyer competing with you for the same home.

Some Lenders Use Pre-Approved and Pre-Qualified Interchangeably.

They really should not. It confuses consumers. But no matter what they call it, when you make an offer on a house, an authentic pre-approval will confirm that your in-depth paperwork has actually been submitted to the lender.

WHERE TO GO FOR A LOAN

Tip #17 — Using a Traditional Bank: Leveraging an Existing Relationship

Banks are known as "direct lenders" because they have the money to fund their own loans. The main tip here is that if you have a strong, existing relationship with a particular bank, if you have an account or two there, and like the idea of a brick-and-mortar institution, a bank may be the way to go. It is sometimes considered to be one-stop shopping, with everything, and everyone, under one roof. And, because of your existing relationship, they can often find ways to incentivize you with discounted fees and favorable interest rates.

On the flip side, a bank usually can only offer a limited choice of in-house loan products and interest rates. It cannot necessarily shop around for you and find the best deal on the open market. Being conservative by nature, banks can also present a challenge if you have some problems with your credit history; sometimes even minor ones.

Tip #18 — Using a Mortgage Broker: Comparison Shopping Extraordinaire

Mortgage brokers are essentially "middlemen" who deal with a number of financial institutions all over the country. Brokers have the ability to shop around for the best interest rates and mortgage products for you, especially if you have a credit problem in your history. They often have more flexibility in negotiating too. A broker can save you a great deal of time by comparison shopping among lenders.

On the flip side, because they do not work for the bank that ultimately funds your loan, they may have less control over the underwriting process than a bank (direct lender) does.

Tip #19   Using a Combination of Bank and Broker: A Blend of Both

There are some lenders that function as both a bank (direct lender) and a broker (middleman). They can fund their own loans like a bank, but they can also shop for the best products and interest rates on the open market. These types of lenders can be a good compromise but will still have some of the same limitations that regular banks or brokers have.

TYPES OF LOANS

Tip #20   Conventional Fixed Rate Loans: The Most Common

Conventional loans make up the majority of home loans in the United States. They are not backed or insured by government agencies. This means that the loans are riskier for the lender. If you default on the loan, the lender has no insurance to back it up. It is their loss. So, the guidelines are stricter.

For buyers with a steady income, an ability to make a down payment (preferably at least 20%), and a decent credit score, conventional loans can provide a reasonably low, "fixed" monthly payment for the entire length of the loan; so, you will always know what the monthly payment will be — no matter what happens in the economy or with rising interest rates.

The amount of your payment depends not only on the interest rate but largely on the term of the loan; or, the *length* of time in which you choose to pay it off. You can do a fifteen-, twenty-, twenty-five-, or thirty-year mortgage. The shorter the term of your loan, the higher the monthly payment will be. The longer the loan period, the lower the monthly payment will be. As you can imagine, thirty-year loans are very popular because it lowers the monthly payment. That is the upside to the buyer/borrower. But the upside to the *lender* on a thirty year loan is that they make more money because they are charging you interest for a longer period of time.

Tip #21 Adjustable Rate Mortgages: Great IF You Are Not Staying Long

Adjustable Rate Mortgages (ARMs) offer very low interest rates for a short period of time (usually three, five, or seven years), which greatly reduces your monthly costs. This period is called a "teaser period." But watch out! When the teaser period ends, the interest rate *resets* itself to the market conditions at that time. If the rates have gone up, you are in danger of dramatically increasing monthly costs — overnight. So be very careful. This type of loan also played a major role in the housing crisis. Many consumers stayed in their homes longer than expected and when the teaser period expired, they did not fully understand what would happen to the size of the monthly payment. When it shot up, millions of people lost their homes due to the inability to make the new, higher payments.

Tip #22 Interest-Only Loans: Rare and Risky

These loans all but disappeared for a few years after the housing crisis. Many people blamed them for the crisis itself. Interest-only loans have returned, but with stricter standards. They have the lowest monthly out-of-pocket costs of all, in the initial phase of the loan, because the early payments only cover the *interest* on the loan. You are not paying down ANY of the principal debt unless you choose to make extra payments.

After the initial phase of the loan has concluded (up to ten years usually), the payment goes way up. And, when you sell, you still owe the entire amount that you borrowed. Be very wary of this type of loan and have a frank conversation with your lender, if you are considering one.

Tip #23 FHA Loans: The Government Helping with the American Dream

FHA loans are insured by the Federal Housing Administration, a government agency. If you cannot pay back your loan, or if you need to sell your house and it is worth less than what you borrowed, the FHA will pay the lender back for you. You can have a credit score as low as 500, but you need to show some steady income, and some down payment — even 3% will do.

Since you are not putting 20% down, they may charge an initial upfront *funding fee* which could be 1–3% of the loan amount. Not to be confused with PMI, this is called *Mortgage Insurance Premium,* or MIP.

DEFINITION: *Point*
You may see the phrase **"a point"** thrown around in your online research or hear it in conversations with lenders. A point is always equal to 1% of the loan amount. When you are quoted a "1-point fee" for any kind of loan or product, it is always equal to 1% of the amount you are borrowing. For example, a fee that is 3 points would be equal to 3% of the loan.

Tip #24 VA Loans: Giving Veterans a Hand Up

VA loans are guaranteed by the United States Department of Veteran's Affairs. These loans can only be gotten through VA-approved lenders. These lenders are protected by the government against loss if you cannot repay the loan.

To obtain a VA loan, you must be a member or a veteran of the U.S. Armed Forces, a reservist or National Guard Member, or an eligible spouse. You can often get a VA loan with no money down at all. But this loan also comes with a one-time upfront funding fee of anywhere from 1% to 3% of the loan amount.

Tip #25   USDA Loans: Not Just for Rural Areas

USDA loans are backed by the U.S. Department of Agriculture as part of the USDA Rural Development Guaranteed Housing Loan Program. Believe it or not, 97% of the geographic U.S. is in USDA loan territory. That means that you could use a USDA loan in the suburbs, too, and not just in the rural areas. A borrower needs to show low – average income *for the area in which they are buying.*

And, they are 100% financed. Meaning, they require no money down and offer better than average interest rates. However, the loans must come with fixed interest rates; adjustable rates are not allowed. They do require the buyer to pay the homeowner's insurance premium, which is not a bad deal when the buyer is receiving 100% financing.

Tip #26   203K Loans: If You Want to Renovate; Two Loans for the Price of One

A 203K is a nifty loan product with two purposes: to buy the home and to renovate it. It is a type of FHA loan that is backed and insured by the U.S. Government. It covers the cost of the renovation, materials and labor and can even cover the cost of temporary housing while you do the work. However, it must become your primary residence. You are allowed to get either a fixed rate or an adjustable rate mortgage.

It is more costly for a consumer to apply for two loans than for one, so this product eliminates the extra expense and hassle of a second loan. You can use it for a major rehab project (called a Standard 203K), or for a home that does not need that much work (Streamline 203K).

Lender Fees: Know What They Are and Ask for Discounts!

Always ask the lending officer or representative what discounts they can offer or what fees they might be able to waive altogether. If they want your business, they will offer you something. If you do not ask, you will not get!

There are various fees associated with processing and funding a loan. Many are small charges, and others are even negotiable. For example, if you have a high credit score or are putting a lot of money down, you might be able to secure a lower interest rate. Or, if you are willing to pay a higher interest rate, the lender might offer you a discount or a credit to offset closing costs.

Here is a quick primer on lender fees. This list may sound confusing and expensive, but again, they are mostly smaller fees and your lender will go over them with you.

Application Fee: A fee to fill out the paperwork and apply for a mortgage. This can sometimes be waived, especially if your real estate agent has a relationship with a lender.

Credit Report Fee: This is a small fee used to pay the credit reporting agency. Lenders sometimes use up to three different credit reporting agencies. This is also sometimes waived if your real estate agent has a working relationship with the mortgage broker.

Processing Fee: This is an upfront fee charged for processing your loan once you have made an offer on a home and commit to using the lender. This is negotiable, particularly if you have good credit.

Origination Fee: This is negotiable and is sometimes not charged at all. The amount is usually expressed as a percentage, typically between 0.5% and 1% of the loan amount.

Recording Fee: This is an administrative fee to record documents, usually with the county.

Appraisal Fee: This is the cost to send an appraiser to the property to evaluate its worth.

Underwriting Fee: This is the cost of the underwriting department reviewing your application and determining if they will loan you the money, and at what terms. The process takes a few weeks. This fee is often 1% of the loan amount but can be lower if you are making a large down payment or are being charged a higher interest rate.

Rate Lock-In Extension Fee: Once your interest rate is set, it is usually locked in for thirty, forty-five, or sixty days. If the closing gets delayed and the rate lock-in expires in the meantime, technically the bank does not have to honor that rate. You are subject to the latest rates — which can be higher than the rate you had locked in. But they usually give you a grace period, especially if the closing was delayed through no fault of yours. And still, some banks do not charge this fee at all, unless the closing is seriously delayed.

Escrow Fee: Your lender often holds some money earmarked for property taxes in an *escrow* account for the duration of the loan. This money is a safety net for the lender if you fall behind on paying your property taxes. And there are fees for this. Costs vary year to year and by area.

Discount Points: You can actually buy a below-market interest rate on your mortgage by purchasing points. A point is always equal to 1% of the loan amount. By buying a lower interest rate, you can save tens of thousands of dollars over the course of the loan (fifteen to thirty years). So, this can really be worth it.

Working with a Real Estate Agent

I recommend taking full advantage of the expertise of a real estate agent. Remember, you do not typically pay the commission; the seller does. So, first off — there is usually no charge to you. But, do not use them only because they are free. Use them for their knowledge, experience, and guidance. There is no downside!

Agents have intimate knowledge of the real estate market and the local inventory, and a deep understanding of the area. They know a good buy when they see it and can help you to avoid a bad buy. They can connect you with all manner of qualified professionals: real estate attorneys, title companies, lenders, inspectors, contractors, insurance providers, day care, schools, domestic help, and more. And they will manage the whole process, which will save you time and alleviate a lot of stress.

Tip #27 — How to Choose and Leverage an Agent: Chemistry and Experience

There are always plenty of real estate agents to choose from in almost any area. There are three main ways to find the right agent for you:

1. Get a referral from a friend who has already bought a home in the area — assuming that your friend had a good experience. A referral is possibly the best way to find an agent because you have real evidence that the process was handled well for someone you know.

2. Talk to listing agents when you visit their open houses. Chat them up and see whom you like and if you click. You are actually interviewing them without them really knowing they are being interviewed. The agent will try to get your business, of course. If you like the agent, take his/her card and tell them you will be in touch. After you have met a few different agents, make your decision.

3. Screen them online. Almost every local agency has a website with a bio on each individual agent in the office. The bio usually shows their years of experience, their philosophy, and any areas in which they specialize. Do not be afraid to call a few of them to see how you like them on the phone and how well they interact with you. Again, until you have screened a few, tell each agent you will be in touch when you are ready to get started.

You Had Me at Hello

How do you know if an agent is the total package and a right fit? An agent might be very experienced and know the market but personal chemistry is also really important. You will spend a lot of time with this agent – probably several months. Does the agent "get" you? Does the agent have an engaging personality? Does he/she get to the point, communicates effectively, and not waste your time?

Do not be afraid to ask a lot of questions upfront. How long has the agent been in the business? Do not assume that a long tenure in the business makes the best agent. Sometimes new agents work harder because they can be a lot hungrier for business. And long-time agents with years and years of experience can sometimes be very busy or, even a little jaded. I also like agents who have lived in the area for a very long time and raised their own kids there or, who currently have kids in the school system. Even better if the agent actually grew up in the area. Those agents have perspective that others do not.

And finally, is the agent tech-savvy? Does he/she get back to you quickly via text, email, or phone – depending on your preferred mode of communication?

Tip #28	For-Sale-by-Owner: Sellers Will Often Cooperate with Your Agent

You may see For-Sale-by-Owner listings online or see For-Sale-By-Owner (FSBO) lawn signs as you drive through town. It is possible to buy a house directly from a seller, but then you will not have the benefit of a real estate agent representing you and looking out for your interests throughout the transaction.

If you drive by a For-Sale-by-Owner sign, or see one online, write down the seller's phone number and give it to your agent. He/she can call the seller and ask if they will cooperate by paying a partial commission on the buy-side. In my experience, most sellers will do this. The seller is mostly trying to avoid paying a *listing* agent. But they want to sell, so they will often work with an agent who brings a buyer. This allows them to pay half the commission that they would have paid if they had hired an agent themselves. To them, it's still a good deal and they will usually pay your agent.

Dual Agency – and Understanding Business Relationships

Dual agency means that one real estate agency is representing both the buyer and seller. The Real Estate Commission (the governing body that oversees agencies) requires that licensed real estate agents make sure that consumers know and understand who is representing them in a transaction. As a buyer, you might think that you are getting "the inside track" by submitting an offer to the seller directly through their own listing agent; believing that you are going "straight to the source." The reality is that it is not always the best thing for you if the real estate agent is representing both you and the seller.

Let us say that you go into an open house and you want to make an offer. You may not have your own real estate agent yet, or even if you do – you want this house and what better way to get it than to work directly with the listing agent, right? Wrong.

First off, it might surprise you to know that the real estate agent hosting a public open house cannot, and should not, give you advice about how to make an offer on the house or for how much. At that moment, that agent is representing the *seller*, not *you*. The agent can discuss general market conditions, the school system, and other unrelated topics. But once he/she begins to advise you on how to make an offer on his/her own listing, he/she has compromised his/her loyalty to the seller. This is considered to be unethical.

In a public open house, the agent is expected to hand you a form that explains these limitations and the different relationships between agents and buyers.

If you decide you want to make an offer, and you want to work with the listing agent anyway – the agent must get written permission from both you and the seller to become a dual agent. You will likely be called upon to sign a disclosure form that shows that you understand this special type of relationship Once all the parties sign it, the agent's loyalties then become divided for the duration of the transaction.

Divided Loyalties

In dual agency, the real estate agent's loyalties are now *equally divided* between the buyer and the seller, even though the seller is probably paying the commission. The agent is now required to represent both parties *equally*, to the detriment of *neither*. The agent cannot help you to get an edge over the seller; or help the seller to get an edge over you. Neither party can be harmed or given any type of advantage over the other as a result of the agent's advice.

As you might imagine, this will have a dramatic impact on the guidance that you expected to get from the agent throughout the transaction. And the seller must also modify his/her expectations regarding the advice — for which he/she hired the listing agent to give in the first place.

Sounds complicated, right? Well, it is. Which is why it is so important to understand dual agency before you find yourself in a dual agency transaction.

The bottom line, in my opinion, is that you will have the best representation if you have your own agent. As for giving up the "inside track", hey — the seller doesn't care which agent brings the offer in. A good offer is a good offer. Regardless, if dual agency comes up along the road to buying a home, discuss it thoroughly with the agent you are working with and he/she will advise you further on the ethics and the pros and cons.

Beginning the Home Search

Tip #29	Start Scheduling Private Showings: Leave Open Houses Behind

There is a point where you should begin to see houses privately. After you have been shopping online and going to public open houses on your own, you will move on to the next level — getting pre-approved for a loan and beginning to work with one real estate agent.

Seeing a home privately is a very different experience than seeing it with a dozen other people in the house. You will see and absorb more of the details of the home and get a far better sense of it. You also need the quiet. If there are noises, inside or outside the home — like creaking floors, clanking radiators, or street traffic — you want to be able to hear them. You will want to discuss the features with your spouse or partner, and your agent, and ask questions without strangers overhearing.

These showings are also a very important time when your agent gets to know your taste, needs, wants, and your deal-breakers. During showings, you are constantly receiving information that is meant to be confidential.

At this stage, there is no longer a need for you to go to open houses, except maybe when you have already seen a home privately with your agent, and you want to go back the next day, on your own, just to see it again.

Technology and Privacy

Note that more homes now than ever are equipped with microphones and cameras — either through nanny cams, security systems, computers, smart thermostats and doorbells, as well as other types of eavesdropping equipment. Be careful what you say (to your agent, spouse, partner,

or friend) inside the property (or even at the front door) if it is something you don't want the seller to hear; especially if it is about how much
you think the home is worth. That would give the seller a real negotiating advantage if you decide to make an offer.

Tip #30   How Not to Overpay: The More You Know

The most important goal of this book is to make sure you *do not overpay* for a home. Even more so, that you make a great buy that will get
you a huge profit when you sell one day. In order to do that, you need to
understand value or *know the market*.

Know the Market – and All the Inventory

Value is the *worth* of something. Of all the homes listed in your price
range, some will be overpriced, some underpriced, and some might be
perfectly priced. So how can you tell which is which and what each home
is actually worth? How can you avoid overpaying? You avoid overpaying
by knowing the market and being a better negotiator than the seller. We'll
get to negotiating a little later. But for now, how can you *know* the market?

The first step is to scheduled private showings and physically walk
through as many homes in your price range as possible. Online shopping is no longer helpful at this stage. Online photos and virtual tours
can be deceiving and never tell the whole story. For example, the wide
angle camera lens used by professional photographers is heavily curved
and that curvature can make rooms appear to be larger than they really
are. Additionally, the way that the photos are taken — the angles of the
shots, will purposely exclude flaws and unappealing features both inside
and outside of the home.

To understand value, it is critical to get inside these homes and see
them up close — the scale, the finishes and the layout. Only a personal
visit tells you all that you need to know.

The next step, with the help of your agent, is to track the progress of those homes — how quickly they sold, and for how much. You will start to see a trend — a pattern with pricing, size, condition, location, etc. When you pay attention to the pattern, it is amazing how quickly you will be able to actually predict which homes will sell and which ones will sit on the market with no offers. I think you can do this after two (maybe three) outings seeing 3–4 homes each time.

And this process will save you time and energy when it comes to making an offer. Let us say you like a particular home, but based on the knowledge that you have accrued, you can tell that it is overpriced and not worth anywhere near what the seller is asking. You decide to make a below-asking offer and are confident that the offer is reasonable and reflects fair market value. But the seller rejects it, or comes back with a completely unrealistic counter offer. You know immediately that there is nowhere to go with this seller. So, naturally you will walk away — not looking back because you know that you were *right* about the value and the seller was *wrong*. This is power. It's both a time-saver and a negotiating tactic because you didn't waste your valuable time with a stubborn seller and you weren't afraid to walk away and that move could make the seller come back to *you*, but on your terms. We will cover how to successfully negotiate this and other scenarios a little later.

"Days on Market" (DOM) and the Absorption Rate

The health of a real estate market is measured by how fast it takes for homes to sell. Real estate agents look at the number of days before a home goes under contract; known simply as Days on Market (DOM). And the Days on Market will be clearly marked on any individual listing. If the *average* number of Days on Market in a whole community is thirty days, and a house that you are interested in has been on the market for sixty days, it can be concluded that the home is overpriced.

However, economists measure how fast homes sell in *months*, not days, and they call it the *absorption rate*.

DEFINITION:

The **absorption rate** is the average number of months it takes for homes to sell in an area. It is a figure used mainly by appraisers and economists. Obviously, if it is several months or more, the market is going down. If it is between one and thirty days, the absorption rate is considered to be one month. That means that the market is going up and buyers are probably competing with one another; making homes sell fast and for top dollar.

Whether it is "days on market" or the "absorption rate," these numbers show how hot (or cold) the market is in a particular community. Ask your real estate agent to show you how fast homes are moving. A good agent will be able to demonstrate this, and the information will prepare you for how fast you need to move on a home – as well as what a reasonable offer will be.

LOCATION:
WHERE TO BUY
WITHIN A COMMUNITY OR TOWN

Tip #31

How to Spot Up-and-Coming Neighborhoods or, That Are Increasing in Value

Bad, or not-so-great neighborhoods, do not always stay that way and can represent a great opportunity for future value if they are on the road to a renaissance. Formerly downtrodden and downright dangerous areas can morph into hip, cool neighborhoods — especially in and around some of the inner cities. The city, or state, might offer financial incentives to developers. Then, the investors line up to buy properties, improve them and sell them for big profits. Regular buyers with vision, who spot this and get in early, will do even better, because they are not *flipping* for a quick profit. If they settle in for a few years, the neighborhood usually only gets hotter and hotter. But more importantly, the rate of appreciation (increase in value) is faster and steeper than in a neighborhood which is already in good shape and just holds its value steadily. The good neighborhood holds its value nicely but the up-and-coming neighborhood can lead you to enormous profits down the road.

If you can spot one of these up-and-coming neighborhoods, you can make an absolute killing if you hold onto it until the renaissance is complete. Even if you do not hold the property until it becomes wildly popular, it will still experience a rapid increase in value along the way. A simple rule of thumb to target ons of these types of areas or neighborhoods is to "follow the money." In what neighborhoods is money being spent — or is planned to be spent?

Signs that a Neighborhood is Up-and-Coming

- Neighborhoods where new or upgraded mass rapid transit is coming soon

- The arrival (or expansion) of a nearby hospital, university, or hotel

- Areas designated by the municipal, state or federal government for redevelopment

- A lesser neighborhood that is immediately adjacent to an expensive neighborhood

- Areas reported in the media as already going through a gentrification process

- An area where big corporations are moving into or are expected to move into

> **DEFINITION:**
>
> **Gentrification** is the rapid improvement of an area that was previously deteriorated. On the upside, gentrification attracts more upscale residents as buyers. On the downside, this process usually displaces poorer residents who have lived there for some time; maybe even for their entire lives.

Tip #32 — Walkability and Rapid Transit: Two Major Perks in the New Economy

Walkable town centers and an accessible commuter transit line of some kind (train or bus) have become more desirable than ever before, to nearly everyone. Communities all over the United States are making adjustments to their infrastructure that encourage walking and biking. Living close enough to walk to a town center is an enormous boost to the value of a home. Buyers do not want to have to get in their car to do everything anymore. They want to know that they can stroll to shops and restaurants, parks, bus or train stations, or to workplaces. Real estate with easy access to town centers and villages has become wildly sought after, and will only get more so in the future.

Tip #33 — A Park Address: Buying On, or Near a Park

Other than the obvious lifestyle benefit, many professionals believe that properties overlooking a park appreciate in value at a faster rate than properties that do not. Some claim that the appreciation rate is at least 10% more than regular homes.

Aesthetically, you get the benefit and the feel of open land (without paying extra taxes), increased light, a nice view, and easy access to recreation. But do basic research on the park. Check if it is well-maintained and safe. But more importantly, make sure it is protected land that will not be built upon or developed in the future. This information should be available at the town hall.

Tip #34 The Double Yellow Line: Buying on a Busier Street

You probably assume that a quiet street is better than a busier one, right? Who does not want peace? I have had many buyers tell me not to show them homes on "streets with double yellow lines." But that is changing! Do not immediately rule out a busy street.

Some buyers want a quiet street to keep their small children safe and away from traffic. Homes on busier streets sometime sell for less than those on quiet streets, depending on the area. However, if there is a fantastic community that you really love but is on the more expensive end of your budget, perhaps the way in is to buy on a busier street.

And not all busy streets are created equal! Some of them are stately thoroughfares with gorgeous homes on them. Still others lead conveniently right into a village or town center which will always be of value. If children are a factor, you can always install a fence — and for dogs, an invisible fence is great.

Additionally, as people age, they tend to want to be around more activity. They can feel isolated on a quiet street, waiting for a lone biker to pedal by every other day. It can get boring. So, you might want to keep your options open. You never know!

Tip #35 Water World: Do the Topography Test

DEFINITION:
Topography is the study of the shape and features of land surfaces.

Why should you care about topography? Because the new climate and weather patterns have changed our world. The flow of water around a home — and how a home sits on the land have never been more important when buying real estate.

You do not have to be a geologist to look at how a home sits on the land around it. Do the simple topography test. Stand outside of the house and look at the land in every direction. If you were rain or flood water, where would you flow first on the street? Would it be to this house or to a neighbor's? Is the foundation of the house elevated above that of the other neighbors' — sitting on top of a small hill or berm? Or, is it positioned at the bottom of a hilly street? In a gulley or valley? Is there a water retention basin nearby or on a neighbor's property? A stream? Do you see moldy grass or concrete in one area, which is evidence that water pools there in wet weather?

Water is Lazy

Water goes to the first place that welcomes it and provides an easy opportunity for pooling. Even if the land appears to be perfectly flat, water has to collect somewhere. So, do not overlook the value and common sense of the topography of the street, property, and neighboring properties. FEMA (Federal Emergency Management Agency, a department of the U.S. Department of Homeland Security) maps are accessible to everyone. But just because a house is not in a designated flood zone by FEMA does not mean that water will not collect somewhere in heavy rain or extreme weather. We will cover more indoor water issues in the inspection section.

Tip #36   Corners, Cul-de-sacs, and Dead Ends

Cul-de-sacs and dead ends are perennially popular among families because the blacktop on the street sometimes becomes an extension of the yard. Kids can ride bikes and play basketball without the fear of being run over. There is no through-traffic to worry about—just a handful of neighbors coming and going.

Corner properties are sometimes overlooked, but do not dismiss them! Yes, many corners are busy locations but some are not. What I call "quiet corner" homes can offer a huge perk, with extra land, which means more yard, and my favorite — loads of extra light because there is usually no house located on one side of the property. I have owned a quiet corner property, myself. I loved it and sold it for a huge profit.

PART 2

Finding the Right Home and Making an Offer

et the game begin! At this stage, you have fallen in love with a property and are preparing to make an offer. Now is the time to move on from *analysis* of the local real estate market to *strategic negotiations* and *direct dealings* with one individual seller. The truth is, this involves some mind games. There is a lot more to making an offer on a home than just submitting paperwork. It's important to get into the mind of the seller; to satisfy his basic needs (but not necessarily all of them) while still making a brilliant buy for yourself. It can be done.

How to Negotiate like a Pro and Be the Winner, Every Time

The number one fear of buyers is of overpaying. This is a legitimate fear. The number one fear of sellers is selling for below market value. These two fears are diametrically opposed to one another. So, how can both buyer and seller be happy and feel like they both made a good deal?

It is very hard (some say impossible) to have two winners in a real estate deal. At the closing table, it can be said that a home was sold for a fair price. But a fair price does not mean that the seller did not leave some money on the table or that the buyer did not overpay.

This book is about making you the winner, every time — and it starts with the negotiation.

Let us say you have found a great house and you are ready to jump in. If you have done your due diligence and know the market, you and your agent will have a very good idea if the asking price is too low, too high, or right on target.

If the price is too high and the house is not attracting other buyers, you will naturally want to come in below asking price. But, how far *below* asking should you go? If there are other buyers circling and there is a bidding war brewing, you may need to pay more than the asking price. In that case, how far *above* asking should you go?

How Much to Offer

Tip #37 — Making a Low-Ball Offer: How Low is Low?

How do you define a low-ball offer? Most real estate agents consider a low-ball offer to be greater than 10% below the asking price. On a $500,000 home, that is an offer *below* $450,000. You might be right to make an offer that low. The home might only be worth $425,000. But the seller may not have come to grips with that fact — yet. Sellers are often in denial about the value of their home and can easily get insulted by a low-ball offer.

If the property has been sitting on the market for a long time, you might make a low-ball offer, just in case the seller accepts it. But it is more likely that he/she will counter your offer. And sometimes, he/she might not even respond at all.

Tip #38 — How Fast Should the Seller Respond to Your Offer: Unwritten Rules

The listing agent (who represents the seller) is ethically required to present any submitted offer to the seller within twenty-four hours. While it is the custom (but not the law) for sellers to give a response within twenty-four hours of receiving it, they are not required to respond within any specific time frame nor, to respond to you at all. When your agent submits an offer on your behalf, there are four possible responses. The seller:

- accepts it
- declines it
- makes a counter offer
- ignores you

When the seller delays responding, or stalls, he/she is taking a very big risk that you will walk away. Why would a seller delay in responding? For any of the following reasons, the seller:

- considers your offer to be way too low or simply not worthy of a quick response
- is expecting an offer from another buyer and wants to see that one before responding
- did not receive your offer in a timely manner
- has family members with whom he/she must consult
- is traveling
- is ill
- is "shopping the offer"

When a Seller Tries to "Shop Your Offer"

Shopping an offer is when a seller uses your offer as leverage to get a better offer out of another buyer. The seller (or listing agent) dangles your offer (usually verbally) to another buyer by saying, *"I have an offer on the table right now at X price. If you can beat that, I will sell it to you."* One way to avoid this is to make your offer available for only twenty-four hours and then take it off the table. You do not have to say this upfront because it could come across as too aggressive. But if you submit and offer and then do not have a response from the seller (or listing agent) within twenty-four hours without hearing a valid reason why, just withdraw the offer and walk away.

Hearing Crickets:
What to Do if the Seller Does Not Respond At All

This is simple. You have three choices: (1) walk away, (2) improve your offer, or (3) let some time go by and if the home is still sitting on the market at a later date, come back with a new (or the same) offer.

Tip #39 — How to Respond to the Counter Offer: The Law of the Middle

The law of the middle is a very predictable pattern. Let us say, the home is listed for $500,000. If you make a low-ball offer at $400,000, you probably expect a counter offer from the seller. From experience, we know that buyers who make below-asking offers usually intend to ultimately come up to the midpoint between their initial offer and the list price, which would be $450,000. It is not an exact science, and the amount the buyer is thinking in his/her head is not always exactly in the middle, but it is almost always close.

More importantly, this scenario is not just about meeting in the middle. It is a way to tell what the buyer is thinking about value at the *beginning* of the negotiation. And this helps sellers — or at least helps the listing agent, who has seen this pattern many times before. So let us assume that the fact that the buyer picked $400,000 to begin the negotiation, shows that the buyer thinks the house is worth $450,000. If the buyer had opened with an initial offer of $475,000, it would show that the buyer probably thinks the house is worth approximately $487,500 — the midpoint between $475,000 and $500,000.

If the buyer offers $400,000, the seller then makes a reasonable counter at $475,000. The buyer then counters back at $425,000. Then the seller says, "$450,000 and you have a deal." The buyer was *always* willing to pay $450,000 as suspected. And so, they usually have a deal. It doesn't always go this way exactly but it does often enough. Understanding this scenario will help you when making an offer.

Tip #40 — Bidding Wars: Paying above Asking Price Does Not Always Mean You Overpaid

Bidding wars are stressful for buyers. They usually result in the buyer paying above the asking price or at least, paying a premium of some amount. But just because a buyer pays above the asking price does not necessarily mean he/she is absurdly overpaying. Why? Three reasons:

1. If other buyers want to compete for it, the home clearly has value at, near, or above the asking price.

2. If there are multiple offers, the asking price was clearly below the market value to begin with.

3. There is a major difference between paying above what was obviously an artificially low asking price vs. paying a *ridiculous* premium. If the buyer has done his/her due diligence, seen lots of homes and understands the value of similar homes, he/she will know where the real value is. The real value may well be above the asking price.

If You Offer Too Much, the House May Not "Appraise"

After your offer is accepted, your bank or lender will send an appraiser to the property to inspect the home for value and to confirm that you did not overpay. If the appraiser thinks it is worth less than what you offered to pay – then it can be said that the house "did not appraise" and the bank will not lend you the money. In this scenario, you can actually get out of the deal and void the contract. Or, you may choose to stay in the deal if the seller lowers the sale price down to the appraisal amount; the value that the bank thought it was worth. We will cover this and other strategies later, in more detail, in the *appraisal* section.

Tip #41 — Paying the Exact Asking Price: When to Give the Seller What He/She Wants

Sometimes the asking price really does reflect the exact value of a home (or close to it). But how will you know? First off, your agent will (and should) know if this is one of those homes. And if you have done your own due diligence by walking through lots of other homes, you will know too. One can tell when a listing is priced right — there is an energy around it and there are signs. It has not been on the market long and there are regular and consistent showings even though an offer has not come in quite yet. It may not be generating an immediate bidding war, but it is clear that other buyers are looking at it; and the list price, by all accounts, is reasonable. It seems inevitable that an offer will be probably be coming in pretty soon.

This is the moment to jump into the water and give the seller what he/she is asking because if you do not, someone else will — and soon. You may be tempted to offer a little under the asking price, just so you can feel good about negotiating the seller down. Every buyer wants to feel this way and it is understandable. But it can be a mistake and cost you the house. Remember, other buyers are looking at the same house and if you delay, you could end up competing with them and driving the price up. Take advantage of being the "first and only" one to step up to the plate and offer full price. It is very difficult for a seller to turn down a full price offer; and super easy to turn down an offer that is below the asking price.

Even if there are no other offers at the moment, what the seller is thinking is that other buyers are still making appointments to see the home and it's only a matter of time before someone makes a full price offer. So, why would they accept an offer below asking price at this point? Of course, the seller could be wrong about that.

If you want to gamble, then go ahead and wait the seller out; thinking you can get it for less if you wait. But if you love the home, you could lose it to someone else who will come in and offer full price sooner.

Tip #42   When Ping-Pong Negotiations Become Absurd

Let us take another house listed at $500,000. You decide to make an offer at $450,000. And let us say that, in your mind, you are willing to come up to $475,000. If the seller makes what could be considered as an unreasonable counter offer, at say $498,000, he/she is not demonstrating a strong motivation to sell. Two thousand dollars below asking price is not a serious counter offer.

Despite this, you may come up with another $10,000 at $460,000 to demonstrate your seriousness. The seller responds once again to you counter — this time at $493,000. At this point, the negotiation is just ping-ponging back and forth and could do so for days, getting nowhere. The seller obviously feels that his/her home is worth the asking price, or close to it. See this scenario for what it is. Put an end to it and show your strength by walking away.

The seller may eventually realize his/her foolish mistake and come back to you at a later date to try to re-open the negotiation. I have seen it happen a thousand times. But chances are that you will have moved on. Even if you have not bought another home, buyers have a funny way of not looking back once they have walked away from an unsuccessful negotiation. This is why a seller is foolish not to take every offer seriously and engage the buyer in a negotiation.

TERMS OF AN OFFER

There are two major parts to a contract: the *price* and the *terms*. The *price* is obviously just a number. The rest of a contract is made up of *terms*.

Terms are provisions, contingencies, or agreed-upon conditions that must be met in order for the contract to be valid. For example, if you state in the contract that you need to obtain a mortgage in order to buy a property, that is a condition of the purchase and it's called a *mortgage contingency*. Getting a mortgage loan is a condition of your offer — a contingency, or a term.

If the bank denies your loan application within the agreed upon window of time, then you are not required to go through with the transaction because you included that contingency in your offer. It's a condition of the purchase that, if not met, *voids* the contract and your deposit money will be returned to you.

Doing an inspection and negotiating any repair issues is also a condition of the purchase and is called the *inspection contingency*. If the inspection does not go well and buyer and seller cannot agree on how to settle repair issues, the contract can also be voided without penalty to either party and your deposit will be returned.

Most of the terms in a real estate contract are time-sensitive. These contingencies or terms must be met by certain dates over the course of the transaction. They are written into the contract and, if not met on time, can termination the deal.

Tip #43 | Terms: Use Them to Protect Yourself or to Improve Your Offer, or Both

Most of the terms in an offer are there to protect your rights as the buyer. And as we've just discussed, some of the conditions allow you to back out of a deal if they are not met — like a successful inspection negotiation or mortgage approval. But they can also be used to make your offer stronger, especially if you are competing with other buyers for the same property.

For instance, if the price you are offering is lower than the seller wants, and you are competing with other buyers, you may opt to remove or limit some of your conditions to make the overall offer more attractive. The following examples are terms that impact the quality of your offer.

Tip #44 | A Term: Amount of the Down Payment and the Mortgage Contingency

As you now know, lenders (and sellers) prefer that you put down at least 20%. This may or may not be possible for you. Putting down less than

20% should not prevent a seller from accepting your offer, but the more money you are putting down, the stronger your offer will be perceived.

The most attractive term that a buyer can employ, without a doubt, is an *all-cash* offer. When you pay all cash, there is no bank involved and no need for a mortgage contingency in the contract at all. For the seller, this means there is no institution presiding over the transaction or dictating anything. No appraisal is required (although you can still order one for informational purposes), there is no danger of a loan not being approved, nor any other problem or delay that can sometimes crop up with a bank. Additionally, for sellers in rush, an all cash buyer can close fast because there is no underwriting process nor any bank-related issues tripping up the transaction.

But let us be realistic. Most people cannot pay with all cash. Most buyers need a home loan. What you *can* do to improve the financing terms is offer a larger down payment or, ask your lender if you can promise, in writing, that the final mortgage approval can be obtained more quickly than what is normal — say, within two weeks. Most banks can certainly do it in three-four weeks. More than four weeks is just way too long.

The longer the bank takes to issue a final mortgage approval, the more nervous the seller gets. So, working with a bank that can turn that process around quickly is a very valuable term to offer. Ask your lender, at the beginning of your home search, how fast they can do it.

Tip #45 A Term: The Closing Date

The average length of time between your offer being accepted and closing is approximately sixty days. Some sellers want to close faster (thirty days); others may want more time, even a few extra months to vacate the property. If a seller has not yet found a new home to go to, or just needs more time to pack up, he/she may want an extended closing period. If you can wait, great. Either way, the closing date is a term and, if you can be flexible on what we call a *fast close* or a *long close*, this will make your offer stronger in the eyes of the seller. However, see the next section on the downside of long closing periods and interest rate lock-ins.

Tip #46   A Term: Long Closing Periods and the Impact on Interest Rate Lock-In

You may be able to accommodate a longer closing date for the seller. But, beware! If you are taking out a mortgage, the favorable interest rate that you have been promised (locked into) could expire with the passage of a certain amount of time.

Here is how it works. Once a seller accepts your offer, your mortgage lender will begin to *float* your loan. This means that the lender will watch rates every day until they see a favorable one and then "lock you in." Once you are locked in, you keep that rate — no matter what happens in the marketplace — whether rates go up or down after that.

But this rate is only guaranteed for a limited number of days. Some lenders guarantee it for forty-five days. If you close in forty-six or more days, your guaranteed rate will expire. And then you will be subjected to a potentially higher rate. Rates could also go lower, but that is a big gamble. If the closing gets delayed just a day or two, and you let the lender know in advance, they will often give a short extension at no cost to you. But longer delays can result in extra charges and fees. So, you need to be aware of that time limit, speak with your lender representative, and plan accordingly.

Tip #47   A Term: Use and Occupancy Agreements or "Lease Backs"

If the seller needs time to find another home and move out, but wants to close and get his/her money from you sooner than later, you can choose to allow him/her to stay in the home for a period of time *after closing* — as your tenants. This means that you will buy the home and close in a normal time frame, but you do not take occupancy. The seller stays in the home after closing. You then become not only the new owner but also a short-term landlord, charging rent to the seller, who has now become your short-term tenant.

In this scenario, a separate agreement is drawn up (usually by the attorneys) called a *Lease Back* or a *Use and Occupancy Agreement*. Why would you do this? It may seem like a hassle. It is a hassle. But again, if you really want the house and are competing with other buyers, offering a lease-back option is a way to allow the seller more time to vacate the premises and is also another term that will make your offer more attractive.

Remember that you will now have to do *two* walk-throughs on the property — one on the day you close and another on the day that they move out, as tenants. See the *walk-through* section at the end of the book for details on how to conduct a walk-through and what to look for.

Tip #48   A Term: Sale Contingency – If You Need to Sell Another Property in Order to Buy

If you need the funds from the sale of your current home in order to purchase a new property, sellers will see this as a negative. It is really difficult to get a seller to accept this kind of a contingency, known as a buyer's *sale contingency*. The obvious reason is that these two transactions are now tied to one another. The success of one depends on the success of the other.

The seller knows that if you do not get to closing table on the sale of your current property, you can back out of the deal on his/her property. The seller would be taking on an enormous risk to accept a liability like this.

Even if your current home already has a committed buyer and is actually under contract with deposit money in escrow, any deal can fall apart at the last minute. If your *sale* falls apart, so does your *purchase*. The seller is then in the position of having to put his/her property back on the market with an added danger of getting less money for it this time around.

If you must sell another property to buy this one, you have two choices. One, is to find a home with a very understanding seller who will accept this term or contingency. This is not impossible; just very difficult. Another is to sell your current home, get the funds out of it and rent an apartment (or a house) until you find a great new home and can make an offer without this contingency attached to it. This might seem like a lot of moving but I have done it myself (as have many past clients) and I can tell you that it is really nice to have all that money in the bank from the sale of your home and to know precisely how much you have to spend on the next one. Additionally, you eliminate the stress of trying to choreograph two closings — a sale and a purchase — on the same day. You can take more time and not be rushed looking for your next great home. This scenario is even better if the market and/or interest rates are falling; the delay on the purchase saves you money and gives you more time to save cash, as well.

Tip #49   A Term: The Inspection Contingency

As a buyer, you have the right to conduct a full inspection of the property — usually carried out by a licensed inspector. The purchase is almost always contingent upon a satisfactory inspection. This is a very important term in the contract. Conducting an inspection is one of the most important steps in buying a home. You should be present when the inspection is happening — not only to see first hand any repair issue that the inspector points out, but to learn the systems, locations of switches, pipes and valves, as well as any idiosyncrasies of your new home. An inspector doesn't just inspect the home. A good inspector teaches you about your new home.

If the inspection turns up more defects or repair items than you can tolerate, and/or if the seller refuses to make any of the repairs of those defects, or fails to give you a credit (some money at closing instead of the repairs), you can usually get out of the deal. (Discuss the same with your attorney or title company.) You have the right to ask for repairs (or cash credits) but if the seller thinks they are frivolous or unwarranted, he/she will push back. And that is when the next set of negotiations will begin. (See later section on *inspections*)

If you are making an offer and competing against other buyers for the same house, you can also modify this term (limit it) to *improve* your offer.. This is an aggressive thing to do and should not be taken lightly.

For example, you can write into your offer that you are only planning to address "major structural problems" with the home such as issues with the roof, foundation, floors and walls. You are limiting the scope of repair items that you plan to address. This sends a message to the seller that you have no plans to nickel-and-dime him/her over minor repair issues like leaky faucets or cracked window panes. This clearly improves your offer and the seller's perception of what it will be like to go through a transaction with you. If you do this, it's important to have some inkling of the condition of the home. Perhaps you have a friend who is a contractor who can look at the house before you make an offer. Or the real estate agent knows the builder who renovated the home and confirms that his/her reputation is stellar. Or you have simply seen enough homes by this point to get your own sense of the condition, even if there are a few hidden flaws.

Tip #50   A Term: The Appraisal Contingency

An appraisal is an estimate of value. When a loan is involved, an appraisal is always part of the buying process and it is done to confirm that the price you are paying is the same or higher than what the lender, that is granting you a mortgage, thinks it is worth. In other words, the lender wants to be sure that you are not overpaying. The bank wants to protect you but also its investment and will send a professional appraiser to the home to check it out. You can (and should) make your offer contingent upon the home appraising for the amount you offered (or more), but not for less. If you are applying for a mortgage, the lender will probably require it to be done.

If a buyer is paying all cash, there is no requirement to have an appraisal because there is no bank or lender, although the buyer can still order one for informational purposes. Professional appraisers are trained to understand property values in a given area. This does not make them infallible. Sometimes they get it wrong and a new appraisal has to be ordered. But having an appraisal contingency is still important to protect you and the lender.

If the property appraises for *less* than what you offered, then there is a problem. The lender will notify you right away to say that the "property did not appraise."

(See Tip #70 for an explanation of what happens when a home does not appraise.)

Tip #51   A Term: Escalation Clause

An escalation clause is sometimes used by buyers in a competitive situation — when you are making an offer on a property that is expected to receive multiple offers. This is a term in your offer whereby you agree to "escalate" the amount of your offer above and beyond any other competing bids. You can escalate it by a dollar amount or a percentage.

Be careful here. Escalation clauses can sometimes work to your advantage, but they can also backfire and are fraught with complications.

When you include an escalation clause in your offer, you are saying, *Whatever the best offer is, I will beat it by a certain amount.* For example, you could offer $10,000 more than the highest bid, or perhaps 1% higher than the highest bid.

It is somewhat complicated for a seller and his/her agent to manage an escalation clause from a buyer. The seller may not even entertain this clause and dismiss your entire offer altogether. Think about it — how can a seller respond to three separate offers when all three parties put an escalation clause into their contracts? This is what makes it difficult.

Even if your offer is the only one with an escalation clause, you have not come up with a purchase price on your own — one that was *your* idea and with which you are comfortable. You will not know in advance how high the other offers are going to be. Therefore, even if the seller accepts this clause, the sale price will be dictated *to* you. When you learn what you are expected to pay for the home, you might agree to that number, at first, because you are caught up in the elation of beating out other buyers. But since you did not generate that price yourself, from your own research and due diligence, you could easily experience buyer's remorse after you have had a chance to think about it, causing you to back out of the deal.

If you are considering this term, then have your real estate agent ask the listing agent *before* you submit the offer, if the seller will seriously consider an escalation clause. If you do not take this first step, you may find that your offer could be disqualified right out of the gate.

How to Submit an Offer

You will likely be submitting an offer through a real estate agent. I have evaluated literally thousands of offers. The quality and level of presentation of the offer package varies from agent to agent. An offer, which can be dozens of pages in length, may well reflect a good price and attractive terms, but the package is sometimes incomplete: sloppy, unclear, lacking a cover letter, and other important documents and/or signatures.

When you think about it, all that a seller typically knows about you is what is in that package. It is all that he/she has to go on when considering your offer.

It is very important, and frankly not that hard, to make a good impression with a well-written and well-presented offer. Not only will the seller take you seriously from the outset, but it will make your offer stand out from others.

Verbal Offers: They Do Not Mean Much

If you want to be taken seriously by the seller, put your offer in writing. Sometimes it is okay to ask the listing agent if a seller would agree to a certain price before you formally submit the offer in writing. But to be taken seriously (and to get a response), write it up. An offer is just not considered to be real until it is in writing. Not to mention that there is nothing for the seller to sign.

HOW TO PRESENT A WRITTEN OFFER

Tip #52 | The Agent's Cover Letter: Makes it Easier for the Seller

An offer packet can consist of over a dozen pages. Your offer will look professional if there is a cover letter. It should be on the letterhead of the real estate agency representing you.

The letter does not have to be long. It should have a few sentences about who you are, what you do for a living, and include a summary of the elements of your offer. A good agent should do this automatically. Confirm that it is being done and have your agent make a copy of the entire offer packet for you.

A cover letter also makes it easier for the listing agent and the seller to assess your offer at a glance; especially when there are multiple offers. It is a basic professional standard that should be met by all agents. Ask your agent if this is his/her practice.

Tip #53 | A Letter from You: The Personal Touch

While some sellers are "all business" and are only interested in the price and the terms of your offer, many others are quite sentimental and care deeply about who is buying their home. This is particularly true when a seller has lived in the home for a very long time and has raised a family there. It's always a good idea to mention some of the specific traits of the home that you love. Telling them that you appreciate the choices they made and the care they took in maintaining the property goes a long way. It's not flattery for flattery's sake. Sellers really enjoy hearing why a buyer loves their home. I have often seen a heartfelt personal letter be the tie-breaker when two competing offers are very similar in price and terms.

Tip #54   The Pre-approval Letter: Always Attach It and Tailor It to Your Offer

As discussed earlier, a seller will typically not take seriously an offer that does not show, in writing, that the buyer is capable of getting a loan. Be sure to have your mortgage representative tailor the letter according to the home you are making an offer on.

For example, if you are approved to spend up to $600,000 but the offer you are making is only for $525,000, have the lender forward you a pre-approval letter with the purchase amount being $525,000. If you use a letter that says that you are pre-approved to $600,000, the seller can see that you can afford to offer more money but you chose not to. Even if the home is not worth more than $525,000, they can still be offended. There is no need to risk offending the seller. Moreover, lenders are used to editing the pre-approval letter to match the terms of a specific property. It takes them about five minutes to edit the letter and email it to you — or to your real estate agent, who is likely writing up the offer.

Tip #55   Proof of Funds: Usually Only Needed If You're Paying with All Cash

If you are in the very lucky position to pay all cash for a property, the seller still needs to know that you are "liquid" enough (have enough cash) to actually purchase the property without a loan. Documented or written proof of funds will always be expected in the form of either a bank statement(s) showing deposit accounts that contain at least the amount you are offering, or a letter from your lawyer or accountant (on letterhead) stating that you have the funds to purchase the property for cash. Sometimes, a listing agent will also ask for proof of funds if you are putting a very large amount down as a deposit — perhaps 30% or more.

Tip #56 — A Copy of the MLS Listing Sheet: Have It for the Record

It is very helpful (and sometimes required) for the attorneys, title company, and lender to receive a copy of the MLS listing sheet along with a copy of the offer. There are also some legal ramifications. Most listings describe the appliances and fixtures included in the sale. At closing time, if any of these items are not in the home, the seller is responsible for providing them because the home was publicly marketed to include them at the outset. A seller cannot market the home as being sold with a refrigerator or a chandelier, for example, and then remove it from the property before closing, unless these items were specifically excluded on the MLS listing sheet.

Other pieces of information that are included on the listing sheet are the annual property taxes, square footage and the size of the lot. In the case of a condo or co-op, there will be amenities described such as access to a pool, tennis court, or other common areas. If any of these items turn out to be untrue or incorrect, you have evidence that the property was marketed with mistakes and the seller — and listing agent — are liable. You then have the ability to take legal action against the seller, as well as the seller's real estate agent.

Tip #57 — The Purchase Contract: Understand the Entire Document

Also known as a *Sales and Purchase Agreement*, it is the main document and centerpiece of your offer. It is a legally binding contract wherein you agree to buy the property and the seller agrees to sell it to you, if all the contingencies in the contract are met. It has all the details of the sale including price, terms, closing date, conditions, appliances and fixtures included, and other disclosures.

The basic contract is several pages long and varies from state to state and country to country. Depending on what state or country you live in, most of the contract is made up of standard boilerplate language. But there may also be custom language that is specific to your offer.

Just because it is a boilerplate document, it does not mean that you should not read every single section and understand every word. It is not difficult to understand, but it requires at least twenty to thirty minutes of your time for serious review with your real estate agent before signing and submitting.

Tip #58 — Seller's Disclosure Form: Always Ask for it – if the Seller Filled One Out

A Sellers' Disclosure Form is a document that has been filled out by the seller and states nearly everything that he/she knows about the condition of the home and property. Some states require that a seller fill one out, but others do not. If one is provided by the seller, you will likely be asked to sign it to show that you have read it and understand it. It is a good document to have.

Some of the issues and/or problems that a seller should disclose in this form include the following:

- Structural defects
- Water control issues
- Plumbing defects
- Electric defects
- Past or current pest infestations such as termites or carpenter bees
- Environmental hazards or building materials including asbestos, mold, or radon
- Age and condition of roof
- Condition of appliances
- Condition of fireplaces
- Presence of underground tanks, septic systems, or wells
- Any past remodeling done with, or without, a permit

- Any nearby or offsite conditions that might affect the use or quiet enjoyment of the property

Tip #59 Lead Paint Disclosure Forms: Get One from the Seller

Lead paint contamination in a home can be a serious health threat, especially to small children. Federal law requires sellers (and their agents) of all homes built before 1978 to provide the following to buyers before they are contractually obligated to buy:

1. The EPA-approved information pamphlet called "Protect Your Family from Lead in Your Home"

2. Any information about the possible presence of lead in the home

3. A Lead Warning Statement, either attached to or included in the contract, which states that the seller has complied with all federal notification requirements

4. A ten-day period in which to conduct a lead paint inspection or assessment. Buyers may voluntarily waive this right. (See more details in *inspection* section.)

Tip #60 Consumer Information Statement: Know Who is Representing You

It is the law that a real estate agent communicate to you, in writing, who he/she is representing in the transaction. Is it you, and you alone? Is it the seller? Is it both? Did you meet him/her in the public open house of the home you are planning to buy? If so, he/she would definitely be representing both you AND the seller.

Because relationships in a real estate transaction can easily become unclear, every single state wants to be sure that the consumer understands them, and is not confused. The only way to do that is by giving the consumer (both buyer and seller) a written document that clearly spells it out. In other words, to whom does the agent owe his/her loyalty and is that loyalty divided in any way?

If it is divided, that is called *dual agency*.

Tip #61   Dual Agency Disclosure Forms

We have already discussed *dual agency*, and what it means, in the section on working with a real estate agent. Note that dual agency is illegal in some states, but legal in others. If you enter into a dual agency transaction in a state where it is legal, there will be at least one Dual Agency Disclosure Form that both you and the seller must sign.

To reiterate, your real estate agent becomes a dual agent if he/she also happens to be the *listing agent* for a home you want to buy.

In fact, it does not even have to be his/her listing. If the home is listed by another agent in his/her office, that is still considered dual agency because the agency, or real estate office, is representing two parties (buyer and seller) in the same transaction.

> **DEFINITION:**
>
> **Agency** means *to represent*. When a real estate agent, or a real estate agency, represents two parties — both buyer and seller — in the same transaction, you have *dual agency*.

In states where dual agency is legal, the law says that an agent can represent both parties. But that agent cannot *advise* either party in any way that would be detrimental to the other. He/she cannot counsel you on how to outwit the *seller* because that would be disloyal to the seller. And once the agent takes you on as a buyer, he/she can no longer counsel the seller on how to outwit *you*, because that compromises the agent's loyalty to *you*. And yet, the seller became the agent's client first — before you — and the seller is also probably paying the commission!

PART 3

When Your Offer Is Accepted by the Seller

Tip #62 — How Your Offer Gets Accepted: Executing the Contract

An executed contract simply means that both parties have *signed* it. When a seller signs the contract, that is the seller's way of accepting it. It is legally binding. The seller is contractually obligated to sell and you are contractually obligated to buy, provided that all the conditions of the contract are met — and met on time. If certain conditions are not met, the contract can become void.

Tip #63 — Earnest Money Deposit: The Good Faith Deposit

Earnest money deposits are not required everywhere. In some areas, they do not exist at all and in others, they are quite common. Also known as a *good faith deposit*, this is a small down payment made at the time the seller accepts your offer. Often, it is a flat fee of $500–$1,000, or anywhere between 1% and 5% of the purchase price.

The purpose is to show the seller good faith; that you are very serious about buying the home and committed to the transaction going forward. You have some skin in the game, as the saying goes. It is not "extra" deposit money. It is part of the overall deposit amount and you will get it back, along with any other deposit monies, if the deal falls apart for legitimate reasons.

Tip #64   Do You Need a Real Estate Attorney? Or is Using the Title Company Enough?

The short answer is no. It is not required that you use an attorney. But I believe that it is very important to be represented by a lawyer in the purchase of a home; particularly your first home. Real estate law is hyper-specific, detailed, and time-sensitive. You may hear that a title company can handle the entire transaction. It can. But while the title company offers legal *services* that allow it to execute the transaction and file paperwork, title agents and paralegals cannot dispense legal *advice*.

There is a huge difference between legal services and legal advice.

Also note that while some title agencies have an attorney on retainer who can answer questions for you, that attorney is often there to protect the interests of the title company, NOT you. If the attorney is not technically representing you, his/her loyalty lies elsewhere.

If you hire a real estate attorney — and I think you should — he/she is representing you and you alone. A real estate attorney provides invaluable advice and protection. And the cost of a real estate attorney is not nearly as expensive as it might sound. Most real estate attorneys do not charge by the hour, but rather, a simple flat fee. The fee is often due at closing, and is part of the closing costs. So why not have your own legal representation? There is much at stake and it is best to have an advocate devoted only to your interests.

I also recommend only those attorneys whose practices are mostly (or all) real estate related. In my experience, attorneys that have real estate as only a limited part or percentage of their practice are not as effective as those who practice mostly, or all, real estate.

It is important that you never take legal advice from a real estate agent. They are licensed to practice real estate; not law.

Tip #65 — The Attorney Review Period: The Right of Rescission

Not every state has an Attorney Review period. Where there is one, it is typically a three-day period where the attorneys for the buyer and seller review the purchase contract that has been signed by both parties. They make changes to it before the transaction can progress. In this period, both the buyer and the seller have the right to back out of the deal without giving a reason and without a penalty.

Attorney review typically begins when the buyer's attorney sends a letter (usually by email) to the seller's attorney and "disapproves" of the contract in its current form. The letter states that if certain changes are made, the contract would be approved.

The seller's attorney then responds, accepting or rejecting those requests on behalf of the seller. Once the two attorneys and buyer and seller all agree to the various changes, attorney review is concluded. With your permission, a letter is sent between the lawyers that states, "Attorney review is now concluded." It can be concluded in fewer than three days or can be extended for weeks, if necessary.

After the attorney review period is concluded, the buyer or seller must use a legal contingency in the contract to cancel or get out of the deal.

Tip #66 — Title Companies and Title Insurance: Clouds on the Title

Sometimes, in the middle of a transaction, we learn that the seller is not *actually* the owner of the property; or that someone else, perhaps a relative, co-owns or has a shared interest in the property. Maybe a divorced man is trying to sell and we learn that his ex-wife's name was never taken off the deed, because they bought it while still married — and she has not given her permission to sell. Or perhaps a sibling is trying to sell the home of a deceased parent without the consent of the other siblings who all happen to share in ownership. A title search will uncover these scenarios.

There are also *liens* that can exist against a property that will prevent it from being sold unless the liens are paid off. These liens include mortgages, unpaid taxes, and even money owed to a contractor. These will also be uncovered by a title search.

Claims or disputes like these are known as *clouds on the title* and, until these clouds have been cleared, they can prevent the ownership of a home from being transferred from one party to another.

If you are borrowing money to buy a home, your lender will require that a *title search* be done to confirm the legal owner(s) of the property and/or what kinds of liens or other clouds on the title might be in place. A title search should be ordered even if you are paying cash. This is done to protect you, but also the lender. Buying title insurance on the property, which is also required by a lender, protects you from any future claims or disputes over ownership. Title fees can be among the largest fees in the closing costs.

The title agency itself is also important to the transaction because it facilities the closing, files paperwork, disburses money, and makes sure that all the details of the transaction are complete and in order. The seller cannot dictate which title agency to use. That is up to you, or the attorney you have hired, to decide. If you have a real estate attorney, he/she will have recommendations because lawyers usually work consistently with certain agencies that they know to be reputable.

DEFINITION:

An **easement** is the legal right to use someone else's land for a specific purpose. Most often, an easement comes up when a municipality needs to access a storm drain, sewer line, or utility pole that happens to be located on your property. Other types of easements might include a path to a public beach or a shared driveway with a neighbor. Even if the easement is not obvious or visible to the naked eye, it will usually come up in the title search. Easements are known to "run with the land"; meaning that, unless removed, they remain in place even when ownership is transferred.

DEFINITION:

Encroachments exist when a structure on your property is partially extended onto your neighbor's land. You are violating the property rights of that land owner. It could be that your garage or driveway is extended a few inches or feet over the property line and onto the neighbor's. It is not always realistic or even feasible to correct an encroachment, so they can be made legal with a written agreement between the two land owners.

Tip #67 — When to Make the Rest of the Down payment and Who Holds the Money

The due date for downpayment funds varies from region to region. But typically, a seller likes to get about half of it soon after accepting your offer, and the other half at the closing table. If you are putting down 20% on a $400,000 home, the total deposit is $80,000. The seller would typically want $40,000 early in the transaction and the other $40,000 at closing (minus any small good faith deposit you may have made).

The money is held "in escrow" in a *trust account* until closing. This means that the money does not go directly to the seller. It is held in the trust account of an attorney, or a title company, and then forwarded to the seller at the closing.

DEFINITION:

A **trust account** is a special bank account that an attorney maintains when he/she holds money on behalf of a client or a third party.

Tip #68 — When to Schedule the Inspection: No Reason to Delay

In some states, the inspection is conducted before making an offer. But in others, it is not conducted until a few days, or even a couple of weeks, into the transaction. If you are buying in a state where there is a three-day attorney review period, it is customary to wait for that to be over before you conduct your inspection. There is no sense in spending the money on an inspection until that window has closed because that window is the most sensitive time period — when either buyer or seller can still walk away from the deal without a penalty.

But it is never too early to interview inspectors, or to research inspection companies. This is also an area where your real estate agent can be of great help. Ask for recommendations. Call at least a couple of them or visit their websites.

Once attorney review is over and you have chosen an inspector, there is no reason to delay getting the inspection done. It is in everyone's interest to know, as quickly as possible, if there are any significant defects or problems with the home. The seller, real estate agents, attorneys, title company, lender, and you will all want to know about the condition of the property as early as possible. You do not want to get too deep into the transaction and come up against a repair issue that cannot be negotiated with the seller, or an environmental issue that you cannot live with.

We will cover specific issues in the *inspection* section.

Tip #69 — The Underwriting Process Begins: A Closer Look at Your Financials

The underwriting process begins once a seller has signed and accepted your offer and you are under contract. Underwriting is the process that takes you from the mortgage *pre-approval step* to obtaining the *final mortgage approval* or *loan commitment.* You can still be denied for a loan, even at this stage. It is uncommon, but it can happen. For example, if there is a sudden change in your income or employment status, it can have an impact on getting a final approval.

Now that you have a signed contract, a professional underwriter (in the bank's underwriting department) will begin to build a file on you, and analyze it against the type of loan you have chosen. The underwriter will probably ask for a few more financial documents in addition to the ones you have already submitted.

Some of these documents are:

- A copy of the signed (fully executed) purchase contract

- Evidence that you made the down payment(s)

- Employment verification

- Income verification

- Photo I.D.

- Documents related to other assets or debt that you may have disclosed

- Renting history, to see evidence that you have paid your rent on time. This is a good predictor of making future mortgage payments on time

Once the underwriter has reviewed all of your documents and is satisfied, you will be issued a *Loan Commitment* (Final Mortgage Approval) followed by a *Clear to Close* (CTC) letter when you are very near closing. Then, the loan can be funded. We will cover more on the final mortgage commitment and the CTC letter in the *closing* section.

DEFINITION:

A **gift letter** is usually required if someone is giving you money for all (or part) of the down payment. This letter states the amount of the gift, the relationship of the person who is gifting it to you, and that the money is indeed a *gift*, and not a loan.

Gift money over a certain amount is taxable as income by the IRS. Check in with your accountant if you are receiving any gift money from a friend or family member.

Tip #70 — The Appraisal: Why You Need It and What to Do if the Home Does Not Appraise

While the underwriting department is evaluating your documents, the lender will also send an appraiser to the property to evaluate the home itself and make sure that it is worth at least what you offered to pay for it, or more. The appraiser will consider the size, condition, and location of the property. Then he/she will compare the home to other comparable (similar) homes in the area. A similar home is called a *comparable* or *comp*, for short.

If the appraiser concludes that the home is worth *less* than what you offered to pay, technically speaking, you will not be approved for a loan on that property. But there are ways to successfully move forward with the purchase anyway.

It Is Not Your Fault if the Home Does Not Appraise.

It's true, it is not your fault if the home does not appraise. You are not a professional appraiser and you obviously felt that the home was worth the amount you offered. If the appraiser determines that the home is worth less, and the property "does not appraise" at the purchase price or above, one solution is to renegotiate the sale price *downward*, to the value that the appraiser gave it. Of course, the seller will not like this and will push back. But the seller may not have a choice if he/she wants to sell it to you.

Another solution is for you, the buyer, to make up the difference between the sale price and the appraised value by putting down more cash. Avoid this unless it suits your needs to put more cash down (therefore, having greater equity in the home). You may have the extra cash to make up the difference. But why should you? There is a reason that banks send appraisers out to the property. It is not just to protect the bank; it is to protect you, too — to make sure that you are not overpaying for current market conditions.

A third solution is for the buyer and seller to meet in the middle, splitting the difference between the two values. This may work if your attorney, real estate agent, and lender all agree that it is a good idea.

Sometimes appraisers just get it plain wrong and mistakenly *under-value* a home. If you, and the professionals around you, feel this is the case, you can appeal to the lender to reconsider the appraisal amount by taking another look at the report and at other, more appropriate comps. They may even send out a second appraiser who is more famil-iar with the neighborhood than the first appraiser. The lender does not really want to lose you as a client, so they will often work with you.

As a buyer, you also have the option of getting a new appraisal by actually switching lenders. This option presents a real challenge because it means you have to start over with a new bank, new paper-work, and a few new fees. As a result, it can delay the closing date and that can be a huge problem for you and/or the seller.

THE HOME INSPECTION

Let us agree on one major point. No home is perfect. Unless you are buying brand-new construction, an inspection will always turn up flaws and at least some repair issues. Even new construction turns up some mistakes or "overlooked" items by the builder. It must be expected. Most repair issues will be evident to your inspector during the inspection — a two-to-four hour evaluation of the home done by a licensed inspector, hired by you, at your expense.

When the inspection is complete and you have received and reviewed the written inspection report, your attorney or real estate agent will ask the seller to make repairs, or give you a cash credit at the closing table — in order to make the repairs yourself, once you own it.

The seller may choose to do neither — make repairs or to give you a cash credit. If he/she does refuse, you can walk away from the deal, assuming there was an inspection contingency in your offer. This is precisely what the inspection contingency is designed to do; to allow you to walk away from the transaction if flaws or defects are uncovered and remain unaddressed by the seller, to your satisfaction.

Undisclosed material defects

A seller is not allowed to hide or conceal any "material defect" from a buyer. If you learn, and can prove after the closing, that the seller deliberately hid a defect from you, you can take legal action against him. If the seller's real estate agent also knew about the defect and withheld it, the real estate agent is also liable.

Tip #71   Keep the Inspection in Perspective

An inspection report can be intimidating; and it can scare you unnecessarily. It is the inspector's job to point out every single flaw, large or small, in the home. As we have discussed, homes are imperfect, even new ones. Do not get overwhelmed by the fear of maintaining a home. Sure, things break. But everything in a home does not break at once. And things are much less likely to break in the first place if you keep up with the maintenance. Some basic maintenance includes: annually servicing the furnace (or boiler), central air-conditioning, cleaning the gutters, not letting paint get to the point of peeling, repairing loose roof shingles, and staying on top of landscaping.

Tip #72   How to Find a Qualified Inspector

It is important that you hire a good, qualified inspector. Not every state requires inspectors to be licensed. If your state does not require licensing, check to see if the inspector is certified through ASHI, the *American Society of Home Inspectors* or NACHI, the *National Association of Certified*

Home Inspectors. These organizations have rigorous training requirements. Inspectors must pass an exam, commit to continuing education throughout their careers, and adhere to a code of ethics.

It is also helpful to get a good recommendation from your real estate agent or attorney. Go online and see if there are reviews for the inspector or the inspection company. Ask how long the inspector has been in the business and how many home inspections he/she has performed.

Most inspections take between two and four hours to complete, depending on the size of the home. The cost is typically in the $300–$700 range. Do remember to ask what will *not* be included in the inspection. For example, if there is snow on the ground, it might be impossible for the inspector to properly evaluate patios, decks, pools, driveways, and the roof. In this case, your real estate agent or attorney should ask for an extension or to hold some money in escrow until those items or areas, can be properly evaluated.

Tip #73   Inspectors Are Generalists: Consider Bringing In a Specialist or Two

An inspector can cover a lot of ground in an inspection and give you some very good concrete information about your new home and how it runs. But sometimes he/she flags something that just does not look right with the electric, plumbing, central air, chimney, or roof. Not being a plumber or an electrician, for example, he/she cannot be sure about the source or extent of the problem. Therefore, he/she will advise bringing in a licensed plumber or electrician for a follow-up evaluation. This takes more time and can cause some delays.

Sometimes, it is a good idea to anticipate this and plan ahead. If you and your real estate agent have an idea that some "issues" might come up around pipes or wiring, heating or cooling, go ahead and book a plumber, roofer, electrician, or HVAC expert to show up on the day of the inspection (while the inspector is there) and take a look at these systems while you are already in the house. Some of these contractors may not even charge you if you plan to hire them later to make the repairs, once you buy the property. This kind of thinking and planning ahead is a huge time saver.

If a repair or an upgrade is needed in one of these specialized areas, you can get the work estimate from the contractor and forward it to the seller along with the inspection report. A good real estate agent should have strong relationships with some of these contractors and should be able to help you in this regard.

Some areas of a home that often require a specialist to evaluate:

- Swimming pools

- Chimneys

- Potentially dangerous electrical wiring such as knob-and-tube

- Sewer lines

- Underground storage tanks, wells and septic tanks

- Roofer

The more investigating you plan for and can complete on the day of the general inspection, the easier the process becomes and the better off you will be.

Potential Inspection Issues

Tip #74
Structural Problems: They Sound Bad but Do Not Panic

It is true that structural issues can be expensive to correct, but they often sound and appear worse than they really are. Structural problems include cracks in the foundation, heaving sidewalks from tree roots, floors that have settled and cause sloping, sagging stairs, an improperly supported main beam in the basement, leaking roof, and loose bannisters.

Most of the time, a master carpenter or a general contractor can make the repairs, and it does not have to cost a lot money. The seller will usually grant these repairs. If the issue is serious, an engineer might need to be called in. Some inspectors are also engineers and therefore will charge more than general inspectors do. If you are buying a property that you think may have some structural issues, it might be better to hire an engineer/inspector from the outset.

Environmental Issues: Almost Always the Seller's Problem

Environmental issues vary from region to region. Most of the common ones will be well known to local inspectors and real estate agents. Ask about them early in your search, as you begin to tour homes in the area. While your real estate agent is probably not an environmental expert, he/she can certainly discuss known environmental issues in the area.

If your inspector sees any signs of an environment-related problems, it is usually necessary for a professional to be called in for a special evaluation.

Some region-specific issues would include certain types of pest, or a mold in a wet climate. Another special inspection is evaluating windows in coastal homes for their ability to withstand a hurricane. It's called a wind mitigation inspection.

Other environmental issues that may vary by region include the existence of underground oil tanks, radon, asbestos, water wells, septic tanks, pests, and flood water.

The seller must disclose the existence of any of these issues (if known) and usually must treat or remediate an environmental problem before closing. But it is still the buyer's responsibility to have the home thoroughly inspected in order to find every possible issue.

Tip #75

Underground Oil Tanks: Never, Ever Buy a Residential Property with an Abandoned or Decommissioned Underground Tank Still on it!

At the time of the inspection, it is crucial to do what's called a tank sweep of the property to check for the presence of an abandoned underground tank — usually the kind that holds, or once held, home heating oil. A tank sweep is an inspection of the grounds around the home. A professional uses something that looks like a Geiger counter to detect any large metal structures underground. It is well worth the small, added expense, because oil clean-ups from leaking tanks can cost thousands of dollars, and in significant spills, tens and even hundreds of thousands of dollars.

This is a major environmental issue and it is the seller's problem, not yours — unless you forget to test for it. There may be a tank on the property that the seller does not even know about. Once you close on the property, any undetected underground tanks become your problem. Oil that has leaked from a tank is considered hazardous waste material. Once the oil has leaked, the soil is considered contaminated.

The tank may be *active* (currently in use to heat the home), and even insured for leakage. It could also have been decommissioned (no longer active or in use but still present on the property). It does not matter. Oil can leak from an active or inactive tank. The tank should be pulled either way.

Do not accept it when the seller tell you that it "has been tested" for leaks and "it passed". Some leaks can go undetected even if the ground around it has been tested and appears clean.

Move ahead with the transaction only if the seller removes the tank altogether — at his/her expense — not yours. If the home still requires oil to heat it (meaning, it was never converted to gas heat) then at the same time that the underground tank is being pulled, the seller must also install an above ground oil tank, usually in the basement. It can be placed outdoors, above-ground, as well. This should all be done before closing. Once you own it, you can always choose to convert to gas heat — or continue to use the oil stored in the above-ground storage tank to heat the home.

Attorneys and real estate agents are actually very good about warning sellers to remove the tanks before they put the property on the market, and about advising buyers not to even consider a home with any kind of underground storage tank on the premises. Never take the seller's word for it, or rely on the accuracy of the seller's disclosure form. Always, always do a tank sweep.

Sometimes, an old buried gasoline tank or abandoned septic tank is found. These should also be removed by the seller, before closing.

Tip #76   Septic Systems: Make Sure It Works and Has Been Well-Maintained

Homes with septic systems are usually found in rural or suburban/rural areas that do not have a municipal sewer system. Instead, homeowners are responsible for the cost, care, and maintenance of their own private septic system. Property taxes tend to be lower in these areas because a public sewer system is a major service which is not provided by the municipality.

A septic system is an underground waste treatment structure. It usually consists of a buried watertight container called a septic tank and a small drain field. It is essential to have the system evaluated by a professional septic company. If not working properly, they can cost tens of thousands of dollars to replace.

One new climate change development is that septic tanks may one day become obsolete in areas with extreme and routine flooding — like some coastal communities. Septic tanks need soil to work. If water levels rise enough, the soil can become contaminated by human waste which not only prevents them from working, but can contaminate the groundwater. Some municipalities around the United States are currently considering spending a great deal of money to start connecting homes to municipal sewer lines and when they cannot, creating what's called a raised septic system (above ground).

Tip #77 — Mold: If There Are Any Signs of It During the Inspection, Test for It

A home inspector will point out any signs of mold in a home. If its presence is suspected, a mold remediation company should be called in to thoroughly inspect and remove it. Removal or remediation should be at the seller's expense.

Both the seller and the listing agent are legally required to disclose the presence of mold, if known. But sellers are not always aware of it. Mold spores in a home can cause minor or major allergic reactions in humans. It can be remediated by removal and/or sanitizing.

Tip #78 — Radon: A Radon Test Should Be an Automatic Part of a General Inspection

Radon is a natural gas that emanates from the ground. It is a breakdown, or a naturally occurring decay of uranium in soil, rock, and water in the earth. Prolonged exposure to this invisible and odorless gas can cause lung cancer. It can enter a home through cracks in the foundation. The remedy for radon is ventilation.

The EPA has determined that a radon level above 0.4pCi/L (picocuries) is "actionable." This means that the presence of radon must be addressed, typically by installing a radon remediation system. It is basically a pipe that goes from the basement — or the foundation — upward, through the roof of the home, dispersing the radon into the atmosphere.

It is usually the seller's responsibility to install one, if radon levels are deemed too high.

Tip #79   Asbestos: If Its Presence is Suspected, Test It and Have It Removed

Asbestos is a mineral fiber once used in building materials such as insulation. It is also a fire retardant. It is often found wrapped around basement heating pipes in older homes to keep the heat in. But it can also be found in old floor or ceiling tiles, roofing, and some cement products.

Asbestos is a known carcinogen and can get into the lungs if it is disturbed by cutting, sanding, age, or in the course of a remodeling project. While the seller is usually required to remove it, you may want to ask for a credit at closing and have the work done yourself once you own it. It is very important that it be removed by a licensed asbestos remediation company so that it is done according to EPA regulations. It is also important to have the company conduct an air quality test afterward, to ensure that there are no fibers left.

Tip #80   Water Wells: Look Out for Lost or Forgotten Wells

Every property has its own history, and usually one that includes several former owners. Sometimes (especially in rural areas), a water well is present on the property. The well may have been decommissioned, abandoned, or even forgotten about over the course of different ownerships.

One can learn of an old well on the property by looking for clues like: a pipe sticking out of the ground, a depression on the land, an old well house, or even an out-of-use windmill. Sometimes, water wells were placed under additions or porches in order to keep the pipes from freezing. And sometimes the town, or neighbors, have knowledge of their existence.

If a well was abandoned (not properly decommissioned), contaminants can get into the ground water and leach onto neighboring properties.

If there is an active well on the property, it is important to have a professional water well contractor test for the water purity. Also, an active well should not be located too close to a septic tank system.

Tip #81 — Pest Issues: Do Not Fret – Most Are Treatable

Pest issues are highly regional in nature, as you would imagine. Each part of the country has its own special brand of bugs that can have an impact on a home. Termites, carpenter bees, carpenter ants, and other wood-boring pests can exist in any wood structure and should be taken seriously. For example, the southern U.S. is known for powder-post beetles and fire ants.

The key here is to inspect for evidence or clues to any damage or possible infestation. This is usually included in a general inspection. Either the inspector is certified to inspect for pests, or he/she will call in a pest control expert to do it during the general inspection. Treatment is best performed before you close or, at least, before you move in.

Tip #82 — Wet Basements: From Efflorescence to Flood Zones

Many basements have what is called *efflorescence* on the inside foundation walls, usually visible in the unfinished part of the basement. It is not necessarily a sign of a bigger problem such as mold. Efflorescence is what happens when some water seeps through concrete, brick, or stone, leaving behind salt deposits that look like a white powdery substance. Unlike mold, it is not a fungus and it can go away on its own.

But mold, on the other hand, is a health hazard and a clear sign of a wet basement. It can be visible or it can hide behind walls. One obvious sign of past water damage that can lead to mold is water marks along the foundation or white chalky marks on drywall in the finished part of a basement. Other signs are rotted wood, a musty smell, spongy carpet or floors, and floor tiles that appear to be lifted.

If a home is in a designated flood zone, this fact is usually known by the seller. It will also be discovered in your title search. FEMA has community flood maps for the entire country that can be found online, on their website. You can also get loads of other information and statistics on river flow, storm tides, rainfall, and topography.

If the home you are buying is located in a flood zone, you will probably be required to purchase flood insurance annually. The amount depends on the level of the zone. There are many different levels.

Negotiating Repairs: Make Your Inspection Report Work for You

The inspection period is a sensitive part of a transaction. The buyer will have a list of items that he/she want repaired or, will ask the seller to give money back at closing to have them corrected. The seller will often disagree with the repair list, feeling that the defects are minor, and that it is expected that an older home will have some flaws or wear-and-tear issues.

For this reason, inspection negotiations can become tense. If they are not handled well, communications break down and the deal could be in danger of falling apart. This is another moment when it is critical that your real estate agent and/or lawyer negotiate successfully on your behalf.

They should be quite experienced in settling conflicts over inspection issues so that both the buyer and the seller are satisfied.

And good communication is key. It is important that they help you to understand which repairs are serious and worthy of a credit, and which issues are relatively minor and to be expected. Ask lots of questions about how they plan to handle these negotiations and how they have had success in the past.

Tip #83 Manage Your Inspector: Take Your Own Notes and Make Sure That What the Inspector Tells You Matches What Will be Written in the Follow-up Report

You should be physically present for the inspection. It is very important to look at repair issues, in person, as the inspector is explaining them to you. But more importantly, when the inspection is over and the inspector provides a written report, you want to make sure that the report matches what was communicated to you, verbally.

When the inspector points out a flaw or a defect, write your own description of it down on your notepad. Then, when you receive the written report, it will be much easier to compare with what you were told during the inspection. Read the report and check it thoroughly. I have seen many examples where a repair issue, or two, was described differently in the report from the way that the inspector communicated it to the buyer during the inspection. It is frustrating when an inspector makes a pretty big deal of certain repair items and then underplays it when it is time to put it down in writing.

The reason that this is so important is because the inspection report is a powerful negotiation tool. You are trying to get the seller to give you money for a repair, or to hire someone and actually make the repair before closing. The seller is not going to want to do either of these things. But they will if they are legitimate. The report legitimizes your request.

The report shows evidence that the issues were found by an objective third party (the inspector) and explained — and even photographed — in a written report. So, it is absolutely essential that the written report *supports* the repair request.

The language that the inspector puts into the report can sometimes be unclear, or too soft.

For example, the inspector may have told you that the roof shows clear evidence of "past water leakage". It may not be leaking at the time of the inspection but clearly there was some water penetration in the past. And yet, in the follow-up report, he/she may only write that you should keep the roof maintained and monitor it for leakage, once you become the owner. You may have left the inspection thinking that you are going to get a new, or repaired roof from the seller. But, when you get your copy of the written report, it doesn't support that.

Another example might be when the inspector tells you that the home's (buried) sewer line that goes out to the street should probably be replaced soon because it is corroded, clogged, or compromised by tree roots having grown into them. Then you get the follow-up report which only says that the sewer line should be cleaned out by a licensed contractor in the future. These two messages are very different. It's important to follow up again with the inspector to clear up any confusion. Sometimes the report needs to be partly re-written.

Tip #84
Repairs vs. Cash Credit Requests: Which One to Ask for

When your inspector uncovers a defect and you want the seller to address it — you have two choices:

- Ask the seller to make the repair before closing.
- Ask for a cash credit when closing and then make the repair yourself, with your own contractor or handyman.

I am a fan of the cash credit at closing.

If you ask the seller to make the repair before closing, he/she may not make the repair to your satisfaction. It is not that the seller purposely plans to do cheap or shoddy work. But at this stage, it is typical for the seller to have *emotionally* moved on even though the closing has not yet taken place. For the seller, it has probably been about a year of planning and preparation to get to this stage. The seller is probably exhausted and maybe even a little angry about having to do more. He/she may be cranky and thinking negative thoughts — that perhaps you got the better end of the deal and that, as it is, he/she is selling the home for less than it's worth; at below market value. And now the seller is asked to make more repairs. It's not a mindset you want the seller to be in while making quality repairs.

At this stage, most sellers just wants the transaction to be over. If you get a cash credit at closing, you get to choose who does the work, oversee it yourself, and be sure that it is done properly.

Tip #85 — A Long List of Repair Requests?: Try Asking for a Global Credit

As we have discussed, sellers do not respond well to a long list of repair requests from a buyer. It usually triggers an initial anger response as soon as they read the list. When they read it a second time, they may calm down a bit, realizing that at least some (if not most or all) of the repair items are actually legitimate. But still, they do not like it and it often throws the transaction into conflict mode. Hopefully, this conflict stage is temporary and can be resolved.

The seller and his/her team (the listing agent and maybe even the seller's attorney) will debate the legitimacy of several, if not all, of the items that you raised. The seller may agree to some repairs, but not all. And then, an item-by-item response will be written and sent back to you.

When you read the seller's response, your initial response may also be one of anger. You may say things like: *Who does this seller think he/she is? How can he/she just say no to these items? These are real repair issues; isn't he/she required to address them? Why should I buy a flawed product? Are they trying to sell me a lemon?*

You can see why this part of the transaction can become tense, and how the deal can become vulnerable — just when you thought things were going great.

The Global Credit

A very effective way to diffuse the tension, resolve the conflict and still get what you want, is to ask for a *global credit*. A global credit is one general, round dollar amount that would satisfy you by covering some, most, or all of the repairs on your list. It satisfies the seller because there is no more need to argue back and forth, debating the validity of the repairs — or to call in professionals to get estimates for the repairs. The itemized repair list is dropped from the conversation altogether. What you are now saying is: *Let us not argue back and forth about the merits of each item. Just give me a mutually agreed-upon lump sum of money and I will spend it my way.*

The seller will usually like the idea because he/she:

- is no longer being asked to make any repairs
- was probably prepared to give you some monies anyway
- can move on with the transaction and to the closing table
- has no need to argue anymore

The only challenge that remains is agreeing on the amount of the global credit.

Repairs that Often Must Be Made before Closing

Some repairs must be done, or somehow addressed, by the seller before closing because they may be environmental in nature and therefore, present a safety hazard. They may also need to be addressed before closing because your insurance carrier or mortgage lender require it, in order to secure the insurance policy or loan.

Some of these types of issues can include:

- Presence of knob-and-tube electrical wiring (which can be active or inactive but either way, it should be removed)

- Radon level in the basement that is higher than allowed

- Presence of an underground oil or gasoline tank (which can be active or inactive but either way, should be removed. Septic tanks are a separate issue — (see section on *septic tanks*)

- Presence of asbestos (which can be removed or sometimes left in place but wrapped/enclosed)

- Presence of mold

- Pest infestation

In any of these cases, if the seller addresses the remediation, it is imperative to get written documentation, prior to closing, that the work was completed by a licensed and insured contractor.

Tip #86 It Ain't Broke: But it is "Past Its Useful Life"

Inspectors often use the term "past its useful life" to describe the condition of an appliance, roof, furnace, or other item. This means that a replacement will be necessary in the future — it might be a few months or a few years. This phrase could easily be interpreted by you as something that the seller should fix right now, or at least provide a cash credit.

But the seller will almost always push back on this, stating, "It ain't broke." He/she will almost inevitably say: *The roof is not leaking and works fine! Or, the furnace is working and producing heat. Why should I replace it?*

This is a common conflict between buyer and seller and when it arises, you have a choice to make about whether to let it go or fight for a repair or credit. If you really want the repair and feel that you deserve it, this is the moment when the professionals representing you (real estate agent and attorney) need to pull out their very best negotiating skills and use them on your behalf.

Here are some options to further that goal:

- Ask for a specialist to come in and give a detailed report on the condition to confirm how much life is really left in the item. There is no downside to this other than delaying the forward progress of the deal a little bit.

- Make a big deal about how you will agree to let this item go — and then try to leverage that goodwill to win on another repair request that is more important to you. This strategy has a very high success rate.

- Threaten to walk away from the deal altogether if you do not get what you want. Do this only if you are truly prepared to walk away; in case the seller calls your bluff! This has about a 50/50 success rate. Some sellers will not budge on principal. But other sellers will not want to risk losing you as a buyer — having to put the house back on the market all over again. This type of seller will usually give in just to keep the deal together and get to the closing table.

- Let this one item go, and instead, ask for a global credit for *all* the necessary repairs in the home.

Preparing to Close

Tip #87   Final Mortgage Commitment: What to Avoid in the Period before Closing

The final mortgage commitment (also known as the *loan commitment*) allows the actual closing process to *begin*. This letter shows that you have submitted and completed all the documents that your lender has asked for throughout the transaction. The lender has reviewed them and is satisfied. The appraisal has been completed. The inspection is done and any repair issues have been negotiated.

In this window of time, it is very important that no major changes take place that may affect your finances.

If there is a sudden or significant change in your financial status, it could really disrupt the mortgage approval process. Some examples include:

- Making another major purchase (especially one that requires applying for a loan, like a car)
- Quitting or changing jobs
- Filing for divorce
- Getting sued
- Being asked to pay child support

If any of these, or similar events should occur, they may have a significant impact upon your ability to pay back the home loan. The bank or lender will likely send your file back to the underwriting department for a new review. It is possible that the lender could deny you the loan. At the very least, it would delay the borrowing process.

Assuming there are no major changes to your finances in this window, there are now two more requirements to be met before closing — one by the seller and one by the buyer.

Closing Costs

There are some one-time fees that are due when you close on a home. Most are lender-related such as title insurance, pre-paid property taxes, as well as some others like the attorney fee. Closing costs are typically between 2-5% of the amount of the loan. For a $200,000 loan, closing costs would be somewhere between $4,000-$10,000. If you do not have enough money to pay the closing costs, some lenders will allow you to fold the closing costs into the loan; essentially financing them. However, by doing that, you will be paying interest on the closing costs in addition to the loan itself. Over the course of the loan, that can really add up.

Paying Your Property Taxes

On closing day, the lender will open an escrow account for you and front-load it with some funds from the closing costs that you paid. These funds are largely used to pay property taxes. Property taxes are paid in three ways:

1. On closing day, closing costs will usually cover paying the first couple of months of property taxes upfront.
2. On closing day, the lender will often take an additional 1-3 months (depending on the lender) worth of property taxes out of closing costs, and hold it in the escrow account in the event that you are unable to pay your taxes at any point during your homeownership. It's a safety net to keep you from falling behind, and to protect their investment.

3. Part of your ongoing regular monthly mortgage payment will be dedicated to paying property taxes throughout your ownership. Remember PITI? A mortgage payment is made up of four parts: principal - interest - taxes - insurance. The lender uses that portion to pay the property taxes directly to the municipality or township. You may wish to pay the property taxes yourself – if the lender allows it. But, many homeowners find it easier to have the lender take care of that. And some lenders make it a requirement that they pay it for you.

Tip #88 — Certificates of Occupancy: The Seller's Responsibility

Each town or community has a different name for the type of municipal inspection that is required to take place before closing day. It is the seller's responsibility to schedule this inspection, allow the town inspector into the home, pay for it, obtain the certificate that shows it was completed, and then give it to you (or your attorney, real estate agent, or title company). The seller cannot sell the property without obtaining one.

Some towns only require something called a *smoke certificate*, which means that the local fire department inspected the smoke detectors and carbon monoxide detectors to be sure that there are enough of them, that they have been placed in the right locations within the home, and that each is in proper working order. Sometimes, the seller must also install a mounted fire extinguisher in or near the kitchen.

Still other towns require inspections with other names such as: *Certificate of Occupancy (C of O)*, a *Certificate of Continued Use (CCU)*, or a *Certificate of Continued Occupancy (CCO)*. These inspections are more in depth and are performed by a representative of the building or zoning departments. These inspectors are checking for safety or building code violations such as missing railings, heaving sidewalks, interior ventilation problems, etc. The town will also confirm that the home is built for its current usage — for example, that it was zoned for, and is being used as a single family or a multifamily dwelling.

Whatever the type of certificate, be sure to get a copy of it at the closing table. It protects you, and you will know that you are moving into a safe structure.

Tip #89 Setting Up Utilities

Two to four weeks before closing, you should open up an account with the local (or regional) utility company, for gas and electric services. However, sometimes the utility company will not open a new account for you until the sellers have terminated the current account associated with the home. If the seller has not done this, ask your real estate agent to follow up and remind the sellers. And do not forget to contact the local water department as well.

Utility companies can schedule the switch in service from seller to the buyer as of the actual closing date. So, if you are closing in the middle of the month, you will not be charged for services until the date on which you actually become the owner.

Tip #90 Landscaping, Snow Removal, and Garbage Pickup

If the seller has used contractors for these services, and you plan to hire people for these types of services as well (as opposed to doing these chores yourself), it might be helpful to keep existing contractors in place, at least for the short term, until you have settled in. If you find that you are not satisfied with their services, it will still buy you some time to find and switch to other providers at a later date. The seller's contractors already know the property and are in place. And it will be relatively easy to transfer the contracts or agreements into your name.

Getting Homeowner's Insurance

Almost all lenders require that you have a homeowner's insurance policy in place before you close. Even if you paid cash for the property and there is no loan, any homeowner should carry an insurance policy on the property.

Tip #91   Homeowner's Insurance: The Buyer's Responsibility

You can purchase a homeowner's insurance policy a week or even a month before you close, but it does not activate, or take effect, until the actual day of closing. So, no matter when you purchase it, you are not being charged for the policy until you own the property.

Every insurance carrier has different requirements but the basic information that the insurer will need from you is the sale price, the mortgage amount, the square footage of the home, and whether or not it will be your primary residence. Some carriers will send an adjuster out to the property to inspect it in person. The insurance carrier or broker will advise you on how much coverage you need.

Your insurance carrier (or broker) will issue an *evidence of property insurance* and a paid receipt for one year. Bring this to the closing as proof that you have a policy in place.

Tip #92   Where to Buy Homeowner's Insurance: Brokers Can Offer More Choice

You can purchase insurance through a d*irect writer* (all the major insurance carriers) or, you can go through an *insurance broker* or *independent agent*. A major insurance carrier will only have in-house products to offer you, with no other outside alternatives. But a broker can go to multiple insurance carriers and actually tailor the policy to your exact needs and shop the best rates. Also, many consumers like having a local broker whom they can communicate with in person, as opposed to dealing with a major carrier by phone or over the Internet.

Tip #93   Insurance Coverage in the New Economy: Consider an Umbrella Policy

Most of what your policy covers is *hazard insurance* for the dwelling itself, your *personal property*, and possible financial help with *temporary living expenses* in the event that something happens to your home that causes you to vacate the property and file an insurance claim.

Liability and Risk

While most of your policy is made up of hazard insurance, part of your policy will also cover *liability*. Liability coverage is for accidents that result in physical harm done to persons while on your property. Ask the insurer what amount of coverage you need. This type of coverage is especially important to your insurance carrier if you have a swimming pool, a trampoline, or even certain breeds of dog.

Umbrella Policies

The new world we live in has become more litigious than ever, and there are more lawyers in it than ever. And people sometimes sue for frivolous reasons. Accidents do happen and even a good friend can elect to sue you on the advice of their lawyer or their own insurance carrier. Many insurance experts recommend taking out an umbrella insurance policy, which protects you further by going above and beyond the minimum liability coverage.

If someone injures themselves anywhere on your property, or in your car, or on your boat, there is a stronger likelihood than ever that they will sue for damages and/or reimbursement for medical bills. In some cases, a plaintiff can even come after your future earnings as well as for their legal costs. An umbrella policy can be an important concept to discuss with your insurance professional.

Tip #94 — Replacement Costs vs. Cash Value; and Personal Belongings

Most claims for homeowner's insurance are for *restoring* a home, not *replacing* a home. Let us say, there has been a fire. Statistically, most homes do not burn to the ground. So, the odds are that you are not replacing the home; you are rebuilding or restoring part of it. The same goes for flood or wind damage.

Replacement costs are exorbitant and some carriers will not even insure for a total replacement, especially with older homes. Older homes have unique features like plaster walls instead of sheetrock, pocket doors, and custom moldings. To replace a home with the quality of materials that were used fifty to a hundred years ago is not realistic or affordable for most people in today's economy.

Personal Property

When you are trying to calculate how much insurance coverage you need, do not forget to include personal property that can be lost, destroyed, or damaged. Personal property includes furniture, rugs, art, drapery, televisions and electronic equipment, clothing and wardrobe, and kitchenware. If there is a fire, or some other incident, these are items that will need to be replaced — in addition to restoring the structure itself. Your insurance carrier will ask you to estimate what your personal property is worth and then advise you on the amount of coverage needed.

Tip #95   High-Value Items in Your Home: Add-Ons and Floaters

If you have very expensive, or extra valuable personal property in the home, there is special coverage available to be added to your policy. They are known as *add-ons* or *floaters* to the policy. If you decide to get extra coverage for these items, some carriers will require actual proof of value, while others do not.

Some of these items include:

- High-end jewelry
- Appraised art
- Silver and gold
- Furs
- Wine collections
- Cameras and high-tech equipment
- Musical instruments/recording studio

Tip #96   Reducing Your Insurance Costs

There are different ways to keep insurance costs down.

- Set a higher deductible for claims (the amount you would pay out of pocket before a claim is covered by the insurance policy)
- Use the same carrier for home and auto insurance and get a discount
- Stay with the same carrier for at least three to five years and get a discount
- Pay the full year of premiums ahead of closing

Home Features that Can Reduce Costs

Some carriers will also reduce your policy costs with some of the following considerations:

- Electric, plumbing, roof, and heating that are less than ten years old
- Home has a Central Station burglar or fire alarm
- Home is near a fire hydrant
- A wooden frame home in an earthquake zone (more likely to withstand earthquakes)
- Home has a water leak detection system (a monitor on the main water valve to detect leaks; often connected to the security system)

LAST STEPS TO CLOSING DAY

Tip #97	Cleared to Close: The Final Step in the Lending Process

Once the lender is completely satisfied that you have met all the conditions of the loan, they will send closing documents to you for review. After you review and sign them, the closing can be finalized. If you do not understand the documents, or any language within the documents, now is the time to ask questions — and make sure to ask before you sign.

The lender will then issue a *Cleared to Close Letter* and wire the money to either your attorney or your title company on closing day.

Bringing Funds to Closing

Aside from the wired money from the bank for the loan itself, you will be expected to bring some funds to the closing table, as well. These funds are mostly made up of the remainder of your downpayment but also include the attorney fee, recording costs, etc. Either your attorney or the title company representative (whoever is overseeing the closing) will tell you in advance exactly how much money to bring and in what form – usually a certified bank check or money order.

Tip #98   Final Walk-Through: How to Conduct It and What to Look for

Every buyer should do a final walk-through of the property *on the day of the closing* — not the day before. Your real estate agent should walk through the property with you. The purpose is to ensure that the home and property are in the same condition as they were when you performed the inspection. If there are any new repair issues or previously unrevealed flaws on the property, you have the right to renegotiate and ask for a credit or repair, even with the closing only a few hours away. Your attorney, real estate agent, or title company will help to negotiate any of these last minute issues for you. It is also a good idea to take a photograph or video of the items or issues and then send that to the attorney or title company.

Things to look for in a walk-through:

1. **Kitchen appliances:** As soon as you walk into the house, turn on the dishwasher and run it on the shortest cycle. You want it to run while you are looking at the rest of the home and property. If there is a problem, it will probably be evident as soon as you turn it on and run a cycle. Check that the refrigerator is cold. The seller may have turned the temperature down (or off) when they moved out so turn it up to check if it is functioning. Briefly turn on the oven, and all four, five, or six burners, all at the same time, to be sure that they work.

2. **Bathrooms and kitchen**: Run every faucet in the house (sinks, bathtubs, and showers) to be sure that: they are not leaking, the hot water is on, there is no water pressure problem, or that any of the drains are clogged. Flush every toilet to be sure they are functioning.

3. **Heating and central air-conditioning systems**: Check the thermostat(s) first. Depending on the time of year, turn up the heat or air conditioning a bit to be sure that the system is working and producing the desired effect.

   Note that if the home has more than one zone of heat or central air-conditioning, there will be a thermostat for each zone. So, you may find a thermostat on the first floor as well as the second floor. Check both.

4. **Debris**: Almost all real estate contracts state that the seller is to leave the property "broom clean and free of debris." You might equate debris with "garbage" but almost anything that is left behind by the seller is considered to be debris. Sometimes it is just a worthless item or two. That is not a big deal and can probably be overlooked by you. But if there is substantial debris left behind on closing day, the seller should be required to have it removed before the deal is done, or credit you enough cash at the closing table to have the debris hauled away. Otherwise, you will incur the headache and/or expense of disposing of it after you own it. Still other items are left by the seller because they are quite difficult to dispose of, such as: firewood, cans of paint, stains, and solvents, old air conditioners, a second old refrigerator in the basement, or an old swing set in the yard. The reason is that some of these are considered to be hazardous material that requires proper disposal by local ordinance. So, open every single closet, drawer, and cabinet in the house and in the garage. Walk the exterior of the property, as well, looking for abandoned items in the shrubs like an old tire or heavy broken planters.

5. **Floors:** Previously unseen flaws such as deep gauges and pet stains in wood floors may not be noticed until the final walk-through, perhaps because they had been concealed by a rug when you were last in the home. The seller should have disclosed them nonetheless. But sometimes they do not, or they forgot about them or were unaware of them. If you find major flaws in flooring, you have the right to negotiate yet another repair credit for that on closing day. And considering the fact that it is closing day, making a repair is not realistic and therefore, a credit is more likely.

6. **Instruction manuals and warranties:** Hopefully, for your convenience and as a courtesy, the seller will have left behind instruction manuals for appliances, sprinkler systems, security systems, sound systems, and heating and cooling systems. Also helpful to you would be any certificates of warranty for appliances.

AT THE CLOSING TABLE AND AFTER

Tip #99   At the Closing Table

Those present at the closing, on your behalf, will be your attorney, title company representative, or both. Your real estate agent should certainly attend the closing, but is not required to. Note that the pandemic of 2020 has changed the rules about who is allowed to be physically present at a closing. Sometimes only essential people like the attorneys will be allowed to attend the closing for the purpose of safety and social distancing. These new guidelines may even stay in place after the pandemic subsides if the industry finds that it is more efficient to continue with such protocols. Also, as more and more electronic document-signing is allowed (by the government and the banking industry), closings may become virtual, in the future.

Sellers are not required to attend the closing. Some sellers will want to attend the closing while others will not. They have the choice because they are able to pre-sign their required documents or, give their lawyer temporary *power of attorney* to sign on their behalf.

As the buyer, you will have many documents to sign that day. Most of them are loan documents. But there are all kinds of legal and recording documents to sign. Once those signatures are complete, the actual transfer of ownership takes place.

Perhaps the most important document to review and finalize at, or before, closing is the *closing disclosure* or *settlement statement*

Tip #100

The Closing Disclosure: Make Sure it Closely Matches the Estimate You Received at the Beginning of the Borrowing Process

The settlement statement is a summary document that discloses all charges, costs, and fees associated with the purchase of a piece of real estate. Actually, by law, this document should be sent to you for review at least three days prior to the closing. This is another development in the new know-before-you-owe law. This document also shows that certain fees are to be split (or pro-rated) between the buyer and the seller. For example, you may be closing in the middle of the month and yet the seller has paid the property taxes for the entire month. In this case, the seller is due a credit to be reimbursed for those pre-paid taxes. The disclosure form will reflect that.

As you may recall, you received a *loan estimate* of all your costs when you first applied for the loan. The closing disclosure form outlines the *exact* costs.

What is important here is that you compare the two documents — and that the costs in the closing disclosure form closely match the costs provided to you in the loan estimate. If they do not match, ask why. If there are mistakes or major inconsistencies found, the closing could be delayed another three days.

On a final note, it is very important that you keep the closing disclosure handy as you (or your accountant/tax preparer) will definitely need it when it comes time to file your next set of tax returns. The sale or purchase of a home is a major part of your tax return for that year The closing disclosure form, or settlement statement, is the one document that is needed to file the tax return because it summarizes the transaction completely.

Once all these documents are signed and the title company and lender are satisfied, you will receive the keys.

Tip #101   Call Your Insurance Carrier and Change the Locks

It is recommended that you contact your insurance carrier, or insurance broker, once the closing has been completed, to notify them that it is done and you are now officially the owner. Sometimes, last minute problems can crop up and prevent the closing from happening, even at this point. Insurance carriers know this, so it is helpful to notify them whether the closing was completed — or not!

It is also recommended that you change the locks as soon as possible. You have no idea with whom, or how many people, the previous seller may have shared house keys in the past. There may be friends, family members, and even contractors with copies of the house key.

Glossary

203K Loan: A type of FHA loan that covers the cost of buying as well as renovating a property.

Absorption rate: The average length of time it takes for homes to sell in an area. Expressed in number of months. (Homes in an area that mostly sell in under one month would still have a one-month absorption rate.)

Add-ons: Additional homeowner's insurance coverage for expensive, or extra valuable items that may be kept in the home or, on the property. Also known as *floaters.*

Adjustable rate mortgage: A loan with a very low interest rate for a short period of time called a teaser period. When the teaser period ends, the interest rate resets to current market conditions and can possibly jump up considerably.

Application package: Used primarily when buying a co-op. An in-depth package of informational documents that a buyer provides and/or fills out to submit to the co-op board for approval.

Appraisal: An opinion of value. The appraisal is most associated with a bank or lender. But other entities can also appraise a property for different reasons, including insurance companies, attorneys, municipalities, private individuals and homeowners.

Appraiser: A professional who evaluates the value of a home.

ASHI: American Society of Home Inspectors. An organization that certifies home inspectors. Another is NACHI — National Association of Certified Home Inspectors. These are good resources for the states that do not require home inspectors to be licensed.

Asking price: The amount of money that a home is listed for or, the amount of money that a for-sale-by-owner is seeking.

Assessment: Payment(s) collected by a condo association from individual unit owners to cover a repair or expense not covered by regular monthly HOA fees.

Attorney review: The period of time during which the attorney(s) review the purchase contract (offer) that has been signed by the buyer and the seller. Attorneys often make mutually agreed-upon changes to the agreement during this period. This period is typically three days long and either party can often cancel the deal without giving a reason and without a penalty.

Bidding war: This is when multiple buyers make offers on the same property.

Board meeting minutes: This is the written record of what was discussed at board meetings.

Boiler: Often confused with a furnace, it is the main heating appliance used for homes with water-fed heat such as hot water baseboard or steam radiator heat. Furnaces are used in homes with forced hot air.

Boilerplate: This is the language in a contract that is preprinted and universal to a standard purchase agreement. Boilerplate language is often modified by either the buyer's or seller's attorney in a transaction.

Capital reserves: This is the money set aside by a condo association to cover repairs and other emergencies.

Cash credit: This is the money credited to the buyer from the seller at closing, instead of the seller making repairs.

C of O: A Certificate of Occupancy is a certificate given by a local official that shows that the town has inspected the property and that it may be occupied according to local regulations.

CCO: A Certificate of Continued Occupancy is a certificate given by a local official that is similar to the C of O.

CCU: A Certificate of Continued Use is a certificate given by a local official that is similar to a C of O and a CCO.

CFPB: The Consumer Financial Protection Bureau is a division of the United States Government.

Clear to close letter: Also known as the CTC letter, this letter from the lender confirms that all requirements of the loan have been met and the loan can now be funded.

Closing: This is the last step where the legal transfer of ownership occurs. Typically held in a conference room in the office of an attorney, title company, or even at a real estate agency.

Closing date: This is a term in the contract. It is the date, agreed upon in advance by the buyer and seller, on which the closing will take place.

Closing disclosure form: This is a document given to a buyer just before closing. It discloses the exact and final costs and fees associated with the purchase.

Cloud on the title: This is a lien or judgement against the property that prevents it from being sold unless "cleared." Clouds on the title will be detected in a title search.

Co-op: A cooperative is a form of ownership in a multi-unit building. Unlike a condo, owners are given shares in the corporation that owns the building as well as a proprietary lease, instead of a deed.

Co-op board: This is usually made up of owners who volunteer to serve on the co-op board of directors, which then enforces rules and manages the finances and care-taking of the building or complex.

Commission: This is a fee paid for professional services. In real estate, it is often paid by the seller to the agency that has listed and marketed the home and is then split with the agency that has brought the buyer.

Common elements: These are the common areas of a multi-unit building such as the roof, lobby, pool, and parking lot. Owners share in the cost of maintaining them.

Comparables: More commonly referred to as comps, these are other similar, or comparable, homes to the one you may want to buy.

Comps are used by appraisers, and by you, to help establish value. In other words, to establish a fair purchase price.

Condominium: This is a form of ownership where someone owns a unit in a multi-unit building but also shares in ownership of the common areas of the property.

Condominium association: This is usually made up of owners who volunteer to serve on the condo association board of directors. The association enforces rules and manages the finances and care-taking of the building or complex.

Consumer information statement: This is a disclosure form, required by law, to be given by the real estate agent to buyers and sellers who must read and sign. The form outlines the relationships between the parties and who is representing whom in the transaction.

Contractor: This is a person or company that performs a task or provides a service for a homeowner.

Conventional loan: This is the most common type of mortgage.

Counter-offer: This is a response from a seller when a buyer makes an offer that the seller thinks is too low. Once the seller makes a counter-offer, a buyer may come back with another counter-offer as well.

Cover letter: This is a letter attached to the front of an offer, from either the real estate agent or the buyer, or both. The letter from the real estate agent typically summarizes the offer. A letter from the buyer is typically more personal in nature; a letter of introduction.

Credit history: This is the document that a lender orders which is a record of your history of paying past bills on time and any and all past debt.

Credit score: Also known as a FICO score, it is a score that reflects your ability and likelihood of paying back a loan.

Cul-de-sac: This is a street that is closed at one end.

Debt-to-income ratio: Expressed as a percentage, it is used by lenders to evaluate the level of risk in lending to you. The lower it is, the better. It is calculated by dividing your total monthly expenses/debt by your gross monthly income.

Decommissioned: This is something that is no longer active but has been professionally deactivated. It usually refers to underground oil tanks or water wells and is not to be confused with tanks or wells that have simply been abandoned.

Deed: This is a written legal document that shows ownership of a property.

Depreciation: This is a way to reduce the taxable value of the something due to wear and tear and the passage of time.

Direct lenders: This is a bank or other financial institution that offers mortgages directly to consumers; without going through an intermediary such as a mortgage broker.

Direct writers: This is an insurance agency or company that does not shop around for the consumer. Direct writers offer policies or products from a single insurance company.

DOM: Days-on-market are the number of days that a property has been on the market before receiving an offer.

Down payment: This is the amount of cash that a buyer is offering the seller other than the amount being borrowed. It can be as little as 3%, but lenders prefer it to be 20% or more. Some special loan products allow 0% down payment.

Dual agency: This is when a real estate agent (or agency) represents both the buyer and the seller in the same transaction.

Dual agency disclosure form: This is a form, or forms, that must be signed by the buyer and the seller when one real estate agent (or agency) is representing both parties in the same transaction.

Earnest money deposit: This is a small deposit made by the buyer at the beginning of a transaction. It is not required everywhere. It is also known as a Good Faith deposit.

Easement: This is the legal right to cross or use someone else's land for a specific purpose.

Efflorescence: This is when moisture appears in the form of salt, or a whitish coating, on the surface of a porous material such as cinderblock walls in a basement.

Encroachment: This is when a property owner violates the land rights of a neighbor by building or extending a structure onto the neighbor's land. It is often a fence, a tiny portion of a garage, or part of a paved driveway.

EPA: Environmental Protection Agency is a great resource for information and regulations for any environmental issues in homes and the land.

Equifax: This is a credit bureau.

Escalation clause: This is a term that a buyer adds to an offer whereby he/she agrees to pay a certain amount higher than any other submitted offer. Usually employed in a bidding war. Many sellers will not entertain them.

Escrow: This is the money held by a neutral third party until a property closes.

Executed contract: This is a contract that has been signed by all parties.

Experian: This is a credit bureau.

Fee simple: This is the highest and most complete form of property ownership such as when purchasing a house instead of a condominium or co-op.

FEMA: Federal Emergency Management Agency is an agency of the U.S. Department of Homeland Security. It coordinates the response to disasters that overwhelm the resources of local and state governments. It also provides maps and other information about all flood zones in the United States.

FHA: Federal Housing Administration is a division of the U.S. Government that provides mortgage insurance on loans made by FHA-approved lenders.

FICO score: This is an individual score, assigned to you, that is used by lenders to determine how much risk there is in lending you money. FICO is a data analytics company and it stands for Fair Isaac Corporation.

Final mortgage commitment: This is offered to you by the lender once the home has fully appraised and the loan package has moved through the underwriting department for final review. It is not to be confused with a cleared-to-close letter which is issued immediately before closing.

Final walk-through: This is a last-minute inspection typically done by the buyer and the real estate agent just prior to closing, to ensure the there has been no significant change in the condition of the property since the initial inspection occurred.

Flipping: This is when an investor buys a property and resells it quickly for a profit.

FSBO: For-Sale-By-Owner is a home that is advertised, shown, negotiated, and sold directly, by the owner, to a buyer, without the services of a real estate agent.

Furnace: This is the main heating appliance used for homes with central air. Often confused with boilers which are used in homes with water-fed heat such as hot-water baseboard or steam radiator heat.

Gentrification: This includes repairing, fixing up, or rebuilding homes and businesses in a deteriorated neighborhood.

Gift letter: A letter that the lender will request which states the amount of the gift money, the relationship between you and the giver, and most importantly, confirming that the money is a gift and not a loan.

Gift money: This is the money given to you by a friend or family member to help with the down payment. Above a certain amount, this money is taxable by the IRS.

Global credit: This is one large dollar amount that the seller gives to the buyer at closing instead of the seller having to make individual repairs.

Good faith deposit: This is a small deposit made by the buyer at the beginning of a transaction. It is not required everywhere. It is also known as Earnest Money Deposit.

Good faith estimate: This is the former name of the document provided by lenders (prior to 2015) which estimated the fees that an individual borrower could expect to pay when securing a home loan. The new, more uniform document is now called a Loan Estimate.

Gross monthly income: This is your total monthly income before taxes and other paycheck deductions.

Gross operating income: This is the total potential annual rental income on a property, before expenses.

Hazard insurance: This is the main part of a homeowner's insurance policy and covers damage to the structure of a home.

HOA: Homeowner's Association is the group of volunteer homeowners in a condo or planned community that makes and enforces rules and collects monthly maintenance fees and determines how it will be spent.

HOA fees: This is the money that is collected monthly by the Homeowner's Association to maintain and/or improve common areas of a condominium building or complex.

Home inspection: This is an in-depth evaluation of the condition of a property.

Homeowner's insurance: This is the insurance that protects a homeowner from loss or damage to the property, its value, and even its contents. Liability coverage is for accidents that may happen to persons while on your property.

HUD: The Department of Housing and Urban Development is an agency of the U.S. Government that supports housing and community development.

HVAC: This is the overall system that includes heating, ventilation, and air-conditioning in a home, building, or business.

Income-producing property: This is a property that produces revenue for its owner, from rental income.

Infrastructure: This is the physical systems and structure of a home, or even of a nation, such as its roads and bridges.

Inspection contingency: This is when the purchase of a property is contingent upon the buyer having an inspection performed and having a satisfactory outcome of that inspection. This is a term of the offer that should be included in the contract.

Inspection report: This is a conclusive report written by the home inspector after completing the evaluation of the condition of the property.

Inspector: This is a qualified professional who is paid to evaluate the physical condition of a property. Not all states require that inspectors be licensed.

Insurance broker: This is a licensed professional who collects a fee for advising clients on insurance needs and helps negotiate policies and fees on their behalf.

Insurance deductible: This is a set and predetermined amount of money that comes out of pocket by the policy holder before the insurance carrier pays the rest of the claim.

Interest-only loan: This is a type of loan designed to lower monthly payments. It requires that the homeowner only pay interest on the loan each month and does not go toward paying down the principal.

Interest rate: This is a percentage based fee that is charged to the borrower for the duration of the loan. It is essentially the cost of borrowing money, in addition to paying back the principal amount borrowed.

Interest rate lock-in: This is when the interest rate offered by the lender, and agreed to by the buyer, is set and will not change between the lock-in date and the closing date.

Inventory: This is comprised of all the available homes on the market and available for sale in a given area.

Investment property: This is a property that is purchased for the specific purpose of producing revenue for its owner, from regular rental income.

IRS: U.S. Internal Revenue Service

Knob-and-tube wiring: This is an older system of electrical wiring that is supported by knobs or cleats and encased in tubes. It can be considered dangerous by some insurance companies today and many insurance carriers will no longer issue a policy on a home with this type of wiring.

Landlord: This is a person who rents a property to a tenant.

Lead paint disclosure form: This is a form that sellers are required to fill out, by federal law, disclosing any known presence or documentation of lead paint in a home.

Liability coverage: The part of a homeowner's insurance policy that covers claims for injuries or accidents sustained to persons inside the home or anywhere on the property.

Lien on a property: This is a judgement, or money owed, by the current owner to a third party that may prevent the property from being sold until the debt is paid. It is also known as a cloud on the title.

List price: This is the amount of money that a seller is seeking for a home that has been publicly listed on an MLS.

Listing: This is a home publicly listed for sale on an MLS.

Listing agent: This is the real estate agent who represents the seller.

Listing sheet: This is the public one-sheeter that describes the important features of a property and the list price.

Loan estimate: This is the document that must be provided (new since 2015) by all lenders to potential borrowers which estimates the fees that a borrower can expect to pay when applying for a home loan.

Loan-to-value ratio: Also known as LTV, it is a ratio that reflects how much money you are putting down compared to how much money you are borrowing. Lenders prefer that you put down at least 20% of the purchase price and then lend you 80%, (and 80/20 LTV) but there are many loan products that permit a buyer to put down far less than 20%.

Lowball offer: This is an offer that is considered, by the seller, to be well below the asking price; but is often considered to be more than 10% below the asking price.

Maintenance fee: This is a monthly fee charged to each owner in a multi-unit building or complex such as a condominium or co-op. The purpose is to help cover building expenses and maintain the common areas.

MIP: Mortgage Insurance Premium is a funding fee that lenders charge on FHA loans where the borrower is only putting down 1–3%.

MLS: Multiple Listing Service is a comprehensive Internet database of homes currently listed and available for sale. Most are public but there are MLSs available only to real estate agents and these are considered to be the most accurate and up-to-date.

Mortgage: This is a loan to buy a property. The property is the collateral.

Mortgage broker: This is a licensed professional who brings borrowers and lenders together.

Mortgage contingency: This is when the purchase of a property is contingent upon the buyer obtaining a mortgage. This is a term of an offer that should always be included in a written offer, unless the buyer is paying with all cash.

Mortgage products: These are different types of loans, or loan products.

Multi-family: This is a building that has two or more dwellings in it.

Municipal debt: This is the money owed by a town or municipality; usually for having made large upgrades to infrastructure such as water mains, streets, parks, etc.

NACHI: National Association of Certified Home Inspectors is an organization that certifies home inspectors.

Net operating income: This is the annual income on an investment property after expenses are covered. It is calculated when you subtract total operating expenses from gross operating income.

Open house: This is a short period of time (usually two to three hours) when a home is open to the public for touring.

Passive income: This is the money earned by an owner of a rental property, business, or other enterprise where the person is not actively involved on a day-to-day basis.

Past its useful life: This term is used to refer to appliances, or other items such as a roof, that are still operational and not necessarily broken, but are older than their predicted life span.

Points: One point is always equal to 1% of the loan amount. This is a fee that is paid by the borrower to the lender at closing in exchange for a reduced interest rate.

Positive cash flow: This is when cash flowing into a property or business is greater than cash flowing out.

Pre-approval: This is when a lender issues a letter stating that it has evaluated a buyer's income, debt, assets, and credit history and determined the amount of money that can be borrowed.

Pre-approval letter: This is a letter from a lender, that gets attached to an offer, which shows that the buyer has been vetted by the lender and is able to secure a loan. Buyer has submitted paperwork to the lender such W-2s or 1099 forms, bank statements, tax returns, pay stubs, etc.

Pre-qualified: This is when a lender determines that a buyer is able to secure a loan and for a specific amount.

Primary residence: This is the home where an owner spends the majority of the year.

Principal debt: This is the original amount of money borrowed that does not include the interest that is charged on the loan.

PMI: Private mortgage insurance is an extra payment added to the monthly mortgage payment that provides a kind of insurance for the lender if you are unable to pay the loan back.

Power of attorney: This is an authorization to legally act on someone else's behalf.

Proof of employment: This is a letter or other document that proves someone works at a certain company or for a certain employer.

Proof of funds: This is usually a copy of a bank statement showing that the buyer has the funds to pay for a home with cash, and without a loan. Proof of funds may also be in the form of a letter from an attorney or an accountant, stating that the buyer has the funds to pay for the home in cash. Some sellers also require proof of funds even when a buyer is taking out a mortgage but is putting down a very large cash deposit.

Property taxes: This is a tax on owned real estate. It is the main source of income for state and local governments.

Proprietary lease: This is a lease given by a corporation. A co-op is a corporation which gives shares in the corporation to a buyer instead of a deed.

Radon: This is an odorless radioactive gas that comes from the natural breakdown of uranium in soil, rock, and water. Excessive or prolonged exposure to it can cause lung cancer.

Redevelopment: This is usually seen in urban areas; it is either demolishing and reconstructing new buildings and/or rehabilitating old, deteriorating ones.

Remediation: This means to remedy something. In real estate, it usually refers to correcting an environmental problem like the presence of lead paint, radon, or a leaking underground oil tank.

Sales and purchase agreement: This is a binding, legal contract between a buyer and seller whereby a seller agrees to sell and the buyer agrees to buy.

Seller's disclosure form: This is a standardized form that is filled out by the seller and provided to the buyer which discloses everything the seller knows about the condition of the property. Some states require it while others do not.

Septic tank: This is a tank on a property in which sewage is broken down and drained into a leaching field. Septic tanks are usually underground but may become more commonly elevated in the future due to rising water tables and sea levels.

Settlement statement: This is a document given at closing that itemizes, to the penny, all costs and fees associated with the transaction — for both buyer and seller.

Sewer line: This is the underground pipe that extends from a home that carries sewage waste to the main sewer line in the street in front of a house.

Shopping an offer: This is when a seller (or listing agent) uses the price and/ or terms of your offer to try and secure a better offer from another buyer.

Smoke certificate: This is a document given by the local fire department to a seller that shows that the smoke detectors and carbon monoxide detectors in a home are working and that the home can continue to be occupied.

Stock certificate: This is a piece of paper that represents ownership in a company or corporation like a co-op. Ownership is measured in the number of shares purchased.

Tank sweep: This is a scan of a property for the presence of an unknown or abandoned underground tank for oil, gasoline, or septic.

Tenant: This is a person who rents property from a landlord.

Terms: This is any condition in a contract other than the price. Some terms include the amount of the down payment, and the appraisal, inspection, and mortgage contingencies.

Title company: This is a company that confirms ownership of a piece of real estate, when ownership is being transferred from a seller to a buyer, by conducting an in-depth examination of the property records. The purpose is also to make sure the there are no potential claims on the property by third parties.

Title search: This is when a title company searches public records to see if there are any claims, debt, or liens on a property that would prevent it from being sold.

Topography: This is the study of the shape and features of land surfaces. Topographical features of a property include how the land rises, slopes, or undulates around the house.

Total operating expenses: This is the annual cost associated with an income-producing property to cover maintenance and repairs, utilities, insurance, and property taxes — but not the mortgage payment.

Town council: This is the governing body of a town; usually as elected officials.

TransUnion: This is a credit bureau.

Trust account: This is a special account that an attorney maintains when holding money on behalf of a client or a third party.

Undervalue: This is an opinion of value that is considered to be less than the real value of a real estate property, company, stock, or commodity.

Underwriting: This is a department within a bank or other lending institution where professionals evaluate your ability to pay back a loan.

Undivided interest: This usually refers to the type of ownership of the common areas of a property that is owned by multiple parties within one building or complex. Each owner has the right to enjoy the common areas but also has the shared responsibility of maintaining it.

USDA: The United States Department of Agriculture

USDA loan: This is a type of loan backed by the USDA's Rural Development Guaranteed Housing Loan Program. Borrowers needs to show low-average income for the area in which they are buying.

VA: The United States Veteran's Administration

VA loan: This is a type of loan available to veterans of the United States Armed Forces, a reservist, or member of the National Guard, or an eligible spouse.

Acknowledgments

I would like to thank the hundreds of buyers and sellers who have put their faith in me over the past twenty years. It was the act of working with them that has brought me such joy, as well as the deep experience I have gained along the way.

Buying and selling real estate requires many professionals to carry out transactions at the highest level. I greatly appreciate the advice and guidance for this book from Tim Keefe, the most forward-thinking professional investor and financial consultant I have ever met; James Ashenfelter, a stellar real estate attorney; Geff Sanford, the brilliant owner of Sanford Insurance; John Nevolo, the excellent and ever-patient mortgage broker; and Karen Parziale, an extraordinary public relations professional.

Most of all, I want to acknowledge the two most important people in my life — my son, Jack Severance, and my husband, Bob Severance. They are the center of my universe — keeping life in perspective and bringing joy to every single day.

Made in the USA
Middletown, DE
01 March 2021